Understanding Accounts

KEN LANGDON AND ALAN BONHAM

Published in 2006 by   Capstone Publishing Ltd. (A Wiley company), The Atrium,
                            Southern Gate Chichester, West Sussex, PO19 8SQ, England

                            Phone   (+44) 1243 779777

Copyright © 2006   Capstone Publishing Ltd

Email (for orders and customer service enquiries): cs-books@wiley.co.uk
Visit our Home Page on www.wiley.co.uk or www.wiley.com

Other Wiley Editorial Offices

John Wiley & Sons Inc., 111 River Street, Hoboken, NJ 07030, USA

Jossey-Bass, 989 Market Street, San Francisco, CA 94103-1741, USA

Wiley-VCH Verlag GmbH, Boschstr. 12, D-69469 Weinheim, Germany

John Wiley & Sons Australia Ltd, 42 McDougall Street, Milton, Queensland 4064, Australia

John Wiley & Sons (Asia) Pte Ltd, 2 Clementi Loop #02-01, Jin Xing Distripark, Singapore 129809

John Wiley & Sons Canada Ltd, 22 Worcester Road, Etobicoke, Ontario, Canada M9W 1L1

Wiley also publishes its books in a variety of electronic formats. Some content that appears
in print may not be available in electronic books.

CIP Catalogue records for this book are available from the British Library and the US Library of Congress
ISBN 1-84112-709-4

Typeset in 9/11pt Garamond by Laserwords Private Limited, Chennai, India

This book is printed on acid-free paper responsibly manufactured from sustainable forestry
in which at least two trees are planted for each one used for paper production.

Contents

01 Introduction to Understanding Accounts   1
02 Definition of Terms: What is an Annual Report? 5
03 Evolution of the Annual Report   13
04 The E-Dimension   21
05 The Global Dimension   29
06 The State of the Art   37
07 In Practice   57
08 Key Concepts and Thinkers   79
09 Resources   91
10 Ten Steps to Understanding Accounts   103

Frequently Asked Questions (FAQs)   117
Index   119

Introduction to Understanding Accounts

This chapter considers who can find the annual report of a company useful, including:

» business people;
» investors.

"Money is like a sixth sense without which you cannot make a complete use of the other five."

W. Somerset Maugham (1874-1965), novelist

A company's annual report and accounts is, mainly produced to protect shareholders. The owners of the business, even very small minority shareholders, have a right to look at the financial performance of the business, and its directors and managers, in a way that is reliable and standardized. They also need the assurance of the company's auditors that the report paints a true and fair picture of the affairs of the business. These assurances are sometimes rather empty. In 1990 for example, Asil Nadir's Polly Peck went into administration. Auditors had previously signed off a balance sheet that showed net assets nearly £1bn, but those working on the insolvency discovered a deficit of £384m.

In 2001 Enron, the US pipeline business turned energy trader, filed for bankruptcy listing $62bn of assets, although these later proved to have seen significantly overstated. Immediately prior to bankruptcy the company's shares traded at 61 cents, down from $80 less than 12 months earlier. Arthur Andersen, the company's auditor, was a casualty of the episode. But brokers' analysts had also supported the company, asking too few pertinent questions about its accounting methods, notably its use of some 2800 offshore entities to conduct its business.

The moral of the story is that many companies in the past have appeared to show healthy profits immediately before calling in the receivers.

The information contained in the annual report is useful to many people apart from shareholders. A customer can use the information contained in a supplier's annual report to assess its strategy, to make sure it is likely to remain competitive, and to check its financial situation to make sure that it is going to stay in business. A supplier can do the same, checking from the strategy statements of its customers and prospective customers, how relevant its products and services are to them, and making sure they will be able to pay for them.

Wise managers also look at the annual report of the company they work for with great interest. They look for two things. First, does the company's long term strategy specifically mentions their part of the business? Second, they need to understand how the management accounts, with which they have had to become familiar, are translated into the financial accounts: the ones that are published. Failure to keep an eye on those two things can lead to unpleasant surprises. After all, if your remuneration package includes payments for your ability to earn return on assets, you need to know how the finance department measures it!

Finally, think of prospective shareholders – people who are weighing up whether to invest in one company or another – they should derive a lot of benefit by reading the most recently published numbers of companies inside the sector where they are about to invest.

So, shareholders, current or prospective, salespeople investigating customers, customers checking on suppliers, and many others can learn from and improve their planning and decision making by reading and analyzing annual reports – if they understand them, of course. I mean, have you ever tried to argue with a finance director? They don't play fair. They have at their disposal an army of jargon, calculated (correct word) to wrong-foot any up-and-coming manager. Believe it or not, according to them, you can have huge reserves on the balance sheet and no money in the bank. You can achieve a 20% return on capital employed and go bust at the same time. Even directors of companies can be weak in this finance area, while brilliant at other parts of their function.

So, if you have ever looked at the figures of a company, seen that its reserved profits amount to hundreds of thousands of pounds, noticed that the overdraft is as high as you have seen it and wondered where the reserves actually are, you are not close enough to the thoughts and techniques of the finance department. You need to get familiar enough with its jargon to ensure that for you the annual report is a useful laying out of the facts. If you cannot understand it, the report will remain an obfuscation of the simple principles of business – is the company making money, does its strategy imply that this might continue, and does it have the cash it needs to stay in business and prosper? Welcome to the world of the company annual report.

As a General Motors executive put it, "We are in the business of making money, not cars."

This book is not a crash course in accounting, but it will enable you to make sense of any annual report you pick up. But, once you have read the book, you will have to keep your hand in by using the knowledge and skills you have gained. The best way to do this is to regularly go through an annual report and analyze the strategy and interpret the numbers in the way this book suggests.

02

Definition of Terms: What is an Annual Report?

This chapter describes the contents of an annual report, and considers:

» what the text of the report says about the strategy of the company;
» what financial documents are included.

"Customers – How do they see us?

"Internal – What must we excel at?

"Financial – How do shareholders see us?

"Innovation – How can we continue to learn, improve and add value?"

Robert Kaplan and David Norton, in their book The Balanced Scorecard[1]

Used well, the annual report gives us answers to the questions above. Some people, comfortable with the financial pages, tend to ignore the rest of the report. They argue that the other text reports are mere advertisements for the company and the brilliance of its directors, while the financial pages are regulated in such a way that they represent the truth about the company. However, neither of these statements is entirely true. Companies do use "creative accounting" that sticks to the letter of the law but still paints a picture that misleads rather than guides the reader. On the other hand, those who are less comfortable with the financial side try to make do with the other parts of the report to try to understand the business. But it is of little use to understand the director's view of the forward strategy of the company if you cannot check that the financial position of the company will allow it to implement that strategy. A company, for example, talking about growth by acquisition is less likely to succeed if it is already deeply in debt. Shareholders in the acquisitive dot.com companies suffered badly from this, if they did not check just how big their debts were.

THE CONTENTS OF AN ANNUAL REPORT

The chairman and directors of a company use the annual report as an advertising document as well as the means to satisfy legal reporting requirements. They are unlikely to open with a sentence such as "We made a lot of mistakes this year and have to own up to a performance far below the potential of the business." Scything through the propaganda is possible, however, for one very important reason. Unless engaged in actual fraud, they are bound to stick to the truth, albeit in a sugar-coated form. The "spin" is there but in most cases a little detective work will reveal what we need to know.

Remember also that the key performance measure of a chairman is the ability to ensure that a company's plans and strategy are implemented efficiently. This means announcing what the future of the business should be and then achieving it. This achievement of expectations is a principal concern of shareholders who have, decided on the type and qualities of the company they want to buy. The shareholders acknowledge, of course, that there is a risk that not all of these expectations will be delivered.

It is for this reason that you will, from time to time, hear of profit warnings. A chairman who realizes that the company is not going to be as profitable as he or she led the shareholders and analysts to expect has to tell them the moment the information is clear and the likelihood of underperforming is high.

This expectation is particularly important in the case of the dividend which shareholders have been led to expect from previous performance or a statement of dividend strategy from the board. In order to meet expectations on dividend, the company has to meet expectations on profit and cash. It needs the profit to cover the costs of the dividend and the requirement for the future of the business, and it needs the cash to actually pay out the dividend amounts. Shareholders will not take it in any other form, and a bouncing dividend check is highly unpopular!

It will probably be helpful at this stage to get hold of your own company's annual report. It will illustrate the points we are about to make.

Mission statement

Many companies put their statement of intent, or their mission statement, on the front cover or in a prominent position on the first page. It is a key vision and strategy statement – these days they tend to be shorter and more useful. The reader should study it and use it to test the validity of what comes later. Every strategy statement and plan for the future should echo this mission statement.

Financial highlights

The inside cover and first page normally contain the company's view of their financial performance last year compared to the year before. This can be interesting, but the numbers are often carefully selected to show the company in the best light. If you want a more independent and consistent way of looking at the financial progress of a company, you will need to crunch the numbers yourself to make your own interpretation.

The chairman's statement

This is always a key description of the intentions of the company. It is impossible to predict what will be in any particular statement except to say that the chairman will pick out the critical issues in the recent past and in the future. Often these critical issues are what shareholders have to form an opinion on. The headings below are almost always covered in the chairman's statement:

» last year's financial performance;
» dividends;
» the way ahead; and
» structure and people.

Last year's financial performance

As part of the historical performance, the chairman will normally comment on the main trading issues of the past year. He or she will put them into the context of the economic situation in the main countries where the company does business and mention other factors outside the board's control which have had an impact, normally a negative impact, on the past year's performance.

Dividends

In almost all cases in the chairman's report you will see a statement that conveys the increase or decrease in dividend proposed this year, and which can be read as the board's strategy on dividend in the future. We have noted earlier that the biggest sin a chairman can commit is to give shareholders unpleasant surprises. This is particularly true where expectations for dividend are concerned.

The way ahead

The chairman here picks out the vital issues involved in the next period of trading. Look carefully at this as you are going to have to feel confident that the issue is in reality what will drive performance and that you agree with the strategy suggested.

In most reports the prospects section will reveal what the company believes is its main competitive advantage. Once again you are going to have to decide whether it is a real advantage, and if it is an advantage which is relevant to future prospects. You can do this if you have some insight into the particular industry.

Structure and people

At this stage in the statement it is very likely that chairmen will comment on the company structure and the quality of the company's people. They record their thanks to their people and end with a rallying cry for continuing hard work and success.

Reports of the chief executive and directors

This report will contain a number of matters required by law. It may also include statements from the directors on the position of the company in a number of areas. Fashions and key issues change, of course, and with them change the contents of this report, although the basic contents, as discussed below, are, in the main, laid down by law.

Principal activities

This is, as the title suggests, a short statement of the principal businesses which the group is in.

Results and dividends

This is a full statement of the profit and dividend figures.

Research and development

This outlines the R&D that is being undertaken by the company. Later in the notes to the accounts we will see the actual amount of money spent. From these two statements we will form a view if, for a company of this type, it is spending enough in this area.

Directors

At this point there is a series of items of information about the directors, their resigning by rotation details of their remuneration and share options, and their interest in the company's shares. There are also reassurances about the directors honoring the period of time when they are not allowed to purchase or sell shares. This period coincides with the time leading up to the announcement of interim and final figures. It is important that members of the board do not deal at that time because plainly they have inside knowledge of the affairs of the company that are about to be made public. This would give them an enormous advantage over the rest of the market. In many reports, rather than having the interests of the directors stated at this point, there is a reference to where this information can be found further into the report.

Other

At this point the report of the directors goes into many different areas. They may cover some or all of the following:

» employment of disabled people;
» employee involvement;
» charitable or political donations;
» environmental issues;
» corporate governance;
» internal finance arrangements;
» auditors; and
» policy on the payment of creditors.

Review of operations

This is an important statement from which we derive the company's strategy. The detection of the overall strategy should not be too difficult. After all, the board of a company is responsible for analyzing possible future plans, deciding on the appropriate strategy and then communicating this to all the people who will be involved in its execution. Those involved in the execution are staff at all levels and in all functions. It is necessary that a consistent set of interlocking plans ensures that what is happening on the shopfloor and at the point of sale and delivery fits in with the intentions of the directors. This communication is very difficult to get right, and its failure is obvious to staff and customers alike.

One simple technique for documenting a board's strategy is to use an 'activity matrix'. The review of operations will contain, in some form, statements of the company's products and market segmentation, and we should be able to reproduce this in a simple matrix like that in Fig. 2.1. The harder the exercise is to do, the less well is the board explaining itself probably to shareholders and staff alike.

Activity matrix	Market 1	Market 2	Market 3	Market 4	Market 5	Market 6	Market 7	Market 8
Product 1								
Product 2								
Product 3								
Product 4								
Product 5								

Fig. 2.1   The activity matrix.

Directors' responsibilities

This is a fairly recent addition to the contents of the annual report. It addresses a number of issues. One of these was that there was some confusion as to what the individual responsibilities of the directors were in relation to the publishing of financial information.

To clear this up a form of words was proposed to cover the directors' responsibilities. These words are exactly replicated in a lot of reports. Where there is a variation it is that instead of the statement saying what the responsibilities are, it says that the directors believe that they have carried out their responsibilities. The underlying responsibilities are the same.

It is a timely reminder to us that the figures we are about to examine in detail are based on opinions, best practice, and the judgment of the board of directors. They are not facts in the same way as we would regard, say, logarithmic tables.

Auditors' report

This is also nearly a standard statement, with few particular variations. It is here to record the fact that the auditors have done their job, how they did the job, and what is their considered opinion of the prepared accounts. The significance of the report lies in whether or not their opinion is qualified in any way, particularly if the auditors express doubts about accounting methods, or about the company's borrowings or its survival as a going concern. A qualified audit report is usually a sign of trouble ahead. Even an unblemished audit one is no cast-iron guarantee.

KEY LEARNING POINTS

Lets try to summarize the answer to the title of this chapter in a few words. Companies thrive if they are selling satisfactory products and services which are popular with their customers into markets which have good potential for growth. Their strategic planning should help them to identify those. They then need the capabilities, whatever they are, to carry out the strategy and change it when required. Finally, they need to manage the business in a way that unites the entire staff behind the strategy and keeps everyone in touch with what is required in a changing environment.

The annual report contains all the information an investor or interested businessperson needs to work out and interpret how well the board of the business is carrying this out, the financial information required to see if the finance of the business supports this strategy, and therefore the likelihood that the company will implement the strategy and prosper.

NOTE

1 Norton, D. and Kaplan, R. (1996) *The Balanced Scorecard*. Harvard Business Press, Cambridge, MA.

03

Evolution of the Annual Report

Annual reports arise from the needs of the shareholders to check on the performance of their company. This chapter looks at

» limited companies, bookkeeping and the finance department;
» the role of the auditor.

"It is easier to teach a poet how to read a balance sheet than it is to teach an accountant to write."

Henry R. Luce (1898-1967), founder of Fortune *and* Time
magazines

How the annual report has arrived in its present form represents the tussle between the shareholders and auditors on the one hand, and the company's directors on the other. More and more standards and regulations are brought in to reflect two things. First the changing face and fashion of business, and second the creativity of directors and accountants to maximize the returns they profess to be giving to shareholders.

MONEY, MONEY, MONEY

"Money is the root of all evil, and yet it is such a useful root that we cannot get on without it any more than we can without potatoes" - so spoke Louisa M. Alcott (1832–88). Money is the root also of all commerce, and the starting point of the history of the annual report.

I once was the sales manager for a computer company, and managed to make a sale to a Nigerian businessman. The sale was progressing rather smoothly, when I discovered that he had answered my questions about having the resources to buy the machine very vaguely. He had the resources, assets but not cash. I was eventually paid, through an agent, with a shipload of cement. My problem was to get the cement off my asset list before the month end accounts were calculated and the finance department became aware of what I had done. This one fling with barter taught me not to do it again. Business depends on money, but exactly how it does is a very difficult concept to understand.

In standard economic theory, money is said to have four distinct but interrelated functions:

» to serve as a medium of exchange universally accepted in exchange for goods or services;
» to act as a measure of value, a common yardstick which makes the operation of the price system possible and provides the basis for keeping records;

» to serve as a standard of deferred payments, the unit in which loans are made and future transactions fixed – without money there could be no commonly accepted basis for borrowing and lending and the concept of credit could not play its huge role in the organization and encouragement of business; and

» to provide a store of wealth, a convenient form in which to hold any income not needed for immediate use – it is the only truly liquid asset, the only one which can be readily converted into other goods.

The complexity of money increased enormously with the abandonment by most countries of the gold standard. Up until the 1930s the issuers of banknotes promised to exchange them for a given amount of gold or silver. The depressions of the 1920s changed all that, and paper money is now issued on the general credit worthiness of the country of issue.

To most individuals, money consists of coins, banknotes, and the readily usable deposits held in banks and other financial institutions. To the economy, however, the total money supply is many times larger than the sum total of individual money holdings defined in this way. This is because a very large proportion of the deposits placed with financial institutions is loaned out, thus multiplying the overall money supply several times over.

Without this device and the concept of interest, the economies of developed and developing countries could not continue to grow at the present pace. It should continue to work, at least until we all decide that we want our money back at the same time. Elements of this phenomenon contributed to the 1929 stock market crash. The use others make of shareholders' and bankers' capital is the basis of an annual report.

RAISING CASH WITH LIMITED LIABILITY

In theory, to sell a product you need first to produce it. To produce it you need money up front. If you have money and no great idea of what to do with it, you need to get someone else to use your cash and earn a return. The joint stock company is the vehicle that brings these two things together.

The Joint Stock Companies Act in the USA, as amended in 1855, permitted such companies to limit the liability of their members, shareholders, to the nominal value of their shares. In effect, by applying for a £1 share, a shareholder agreed to subscribe £1 and was not liable for any further contribution in the event of the company's insolvency.

Leading from the joint stock company is the need for a set of rules which managers have to obey in order to give a fair picture of the financial health of the enterprise. The rules are laid down in company law and accounting standards. The auditors confirm that the company's directors have complied with these rules.

The repercussions of the simple idea of shareholder investment are legion. Previously impossible ideas became possible and the idea of trading shares through organized stock markets was born. It is possible to describe the attributes of shares in any way that suits the board and the shareholders. As one example, convertible loan stock is a system whereby the shareholder takes a reduced risk for the certainty of return in the early stages of an investment. Without these devices, long-term projects such as the Eurotunnel would never have come to completion. At its best, the limited company enables risk takers to raise money from shareholders who know that not all of the risks will pay off. This promotes creativity in business without bankrupting the individuals who took the risk. The limited company at its worst enables individuals to walk away from the mess they have created under its protection, and then do it all over again somewhere else.

The company audit at its best guarantees shareholders that the directors of the joint stock company are using their money legally and to good effect. At its worst, the company audit gives shareholders a false sense of security, so that they feel comfortable while risking the loss of their capital. In this respect it can be very similar to the insurance policy which permits the householder to sleep at night while their house is burgled, but then fails to pay out because of a clause in the small print. If you find this difficult to believe, then remember the number of companies that have gone spectacularly bust within months of their auditors agreeing in the annual report that the figures therein were a fair picture of a going concern.

BOOKKEEPING AND THE FINANCE DEPARTMENT

The concept of stewardship followed the invention of the joint stock company to allay the fears of would-be investors. Stewardship involves the orderly recording of business transactions and the presentation of summary reports. This is pejoratively known as bean counting, but can be of great value to the people running the business.

The main principles of what became double-entry bookkeeping emerged in Italy at the time of the Renaissance. They were based on a treatise by Luca Paciolito and reflected the growing complexity of business life. The development of bookkeeping and accountancy reflects the history of commerce.

Bookkeeping has three main purposes – it acts as:

» a check against fraud and error;
» a source of the information managers need to make decisions; and
» the basis for the accounting practices which give rise to the audit.

Whilst bookkeeping can become highly complex, basically there are two types of books used in the bookkeeping process – journals and ledgers. A journal contains the daily transactions (sales, purchases, and so on) and the ledger keeps the record of individual accounts.

As mentioned above, double-entry bookkeeping provides a check against fraud and error. This is achieved by requiring the bookkeeper to enter every transaction twice – once as a debit and once as a credit. For example, the purchase of a fixed asset on credit will require a debit entry in the fixed assets account and a credit in the supplier's account. The subsequent payment to the supplier will involve a debit in the supplier's account and a credit in the bank account. (This reference to a credit in the bank account when a payment is made frequently causes confusion since we are used to seeing a payment shown as a debit in our bank statement. The point is of course that the bank is looking at the transaction from the opposite point of view.) We mention this aspect of basic bookkeeping merely to make the point that the advent of the computer has destroyed this control aspect of double-entry bookkeeping. The computer will make the second entry automatically. The bookkeeper now only has one chance to get it right rather than two.

But, obviously, the computer has also been a great boon for accountants. It has given them the opportunity to process and manipulate large volumes of material very easily. Unfortunately, it has also given them the opportunity to produce yards of meaningless computer printout, which obscures the fact of what is really happening in the business.

Another aspect of the computer and Internet revolution is the opportunity to process and interpret information remotely. Accountants can have access to their client's accounting records on a daily basis. Regular feedback can be provided which is helpful to the business. But it also raises the possibility of fraud and other forms of white collar crime.

The remote processing of data has now been taken to an extreme position. A number of major companies have moved their accounts departments to other parts of the world to achieve cost savings. For smaller companies, accounting can be outsourced via the Internet, with India becoming a very popular provider of accountancy services at a fraction of the price that it's available for at home.

Following on from basic bookkeeping, the accountant will then prepare each month the income statement, which presents the changes that have occurred over the period in question, and the balance sheet, which shows the financial state of a company at a point in time in terms of assets, liabilities, and the ownership equity. Again, this role of accounts preparation is being taken over more and more by the computer, leaving the accountant to play the more valuable role of interpretation. It is true to say that the average businessperson will have a natural understanding of the performance statement – the profit and loss account – but the balance sheet is still a closed book to many. The problem is that a lot of people mistakenly expect the balance sheet to reveal what the business is worth.

Nowadays accountants can and do play a most constructive role in the management of businesses. At least the enlightened ones do – the others just keep the score.

A lot of nonfinancial managers discover late in their careers that a good basis in accounting would have been a boon. Do you know enough about the bookkeeping and management accounts of the business you work in? If the answer is no, put it right – you could be working with one hand tied behind your back.

Kevin Goldstein-Jackson, a private investor and journalist with a good, and very public, track record swears by company reports. "Research is vital," he says, "I take into account many factors in company reports, ranging from the quality of the directors and management to the small print."[1]

ACQUISITIONS, MERGERS AND CAPITAL TRANSACTIONS

Complexity has always existed in businesses. But the volatility and globalization of capital markets has increased it significantly. This complexity has also been heightened by the strategies pursued as a result of fashionable management theories.

During the 1970s, for example, many companies in staid or risky businesses pursued diversification into unrelated areas as a way of improving their image. It reached its zenith with tobacco companies buying restaurant chains and cosmetics companies and with an advertising agency (Saatchi & Saatchi) attempting to buy the high street banking group (Midland – since absorbed by HSBC). The usual rationale for moves like this was that the logic did not matter, because the superior management of the bidder would automatically add value to the target.

The 1980s was the era of 'earn-outs'. This was where an extra price was paid to the vendors in a takeover if profits subsequently met certain profit targets, saddling the merged company with large contingent liabilities that seemed to kick in just as trading turned down. This decade also saw extensive use by acquisitive companies of accounting methods that allowed companies to make excessive provisions in their balance sheets against expected restructuring costs, and then release them to benefit profits when they proved not to have been necessary.

After the early 1990s recession, 'back to basics' became the watchword, with many companies selling or demerging peripheral businesses to improve their balance sheets. Capital structures have also changed. The recent period of low interest rates had led many companies to use debt to buy back their own shares, raising borrowings to do so. This fad may also eventually have to be reversed if trickier times return.

Taxation policy is another driver of capital structures. If a finance minister changes the rules on dividend taxation, for example, you must expect that to alter companies' attitudes to the balance between debt capital and shareholder capital. This leads in turn to what was a fairly rare occurrence increasing in importance – the handing back of surplus cash to the shareholders. We will see how this affects the performance of the company in terms of earnings per share in due course.

This means that nowadays a lot of the presentation and detective work of writing and reading an annual report is about examining the capital structure. Why did the company buy back some of its own shares? How does the financial director deal with goodwill and its amortization?

KEY LEARNING POINTS

The evolution of the annual report is a long and quite complex path; but the root objective stays the same. The authorities continue to try to regulate companies to produce reports that lay open the history and aspirations of the company while at the same time giving a clear statement of the current and future financial position. Meanwhile the companies work within the letter of these regulations as part of their competitive strategy and overwhelming desire to increase their share prices.

NOTE

1 *The Financial Times* March 17/18, (2001).

04

The E-Dimension

The Internet offers challenges and opportunities to make use of published information. This chapter includes information on:

» electronic publication of annual reports, sharing insights and information;
» creating an e-based knowledge centre.

"A distributed system is one in which the failure of a computer you didn't even know existed can render your own computer inoperable."

Leslie Lamport (b. 1941), computer scientist

E-TRADING

Chapter 5 of this book concerns the global dimension; so we will confine this chapter to the impact of the Internet and intranets on matters not concerned with globalization.

One of the writers of this book scared his daughter enormously when he started to use the Internet for investment purposes. She hated the way that her Dad could, all on his own, decide to buy some shares and order them at the push of a button. She just felt that at least if you made a telephone call there was some sort of recording of the voices that could be looked back at to make sure that what had in fact been ordered had been carried out by the broker. With the Internet, there was no such simple device except what the computer programmers of the online stockbroker had put in place. But we are assured that security is first class; in fact far superior to any other means of placing buy or sell orders.

However true or false that is, there has been a huge upsurge in the proportion of share transactions taking place on the Internet.

There are three main reasons for this. First, stockbroking has become very competitive, and online trading offers reductions in costs to the stockbroker that can be, and are, passed on to the investor in lower transaction charges. Transaction charges are an important element in any share deal, and investors are well advised to look for the best deal they can get, in order to maximize the return on their investment.

Second, the Internet not only offers the means of buying and selling shares, but it also offers investors easy access to complex trades such as hedging and spread betting more or less a 7 days a week, 24 hours a day. People therefore make a principal hobby, or even a profession, out of day trading – speculating on the online market in an attempt to make capital profits in a very short time and very frequently. The evidence for their success, it is sobering to realize, is thin. There is better evidence that says that the grand majority of day traders lose money – often very quickly.

The third e-dimension that pushes people towards online trading is the fact that the information they wish to analyze before making a buying or selling decision is available on the same medium. This comes from, amongst other areas, information available on company web sites, access to professional analysts' advice, news-sheets, and forums where like-minded individuals can exchange views.

ELECTRONIC PUBLICATION OF ANNUAL REPORTS

Companies have been publishing accounts on their web sites for some time. In the past this was seen as the provision of information to potential customers and investors, but it was not the primary means of communicating with existing shareholders. In December 2000, in the UK, the Companies Act was amended to allow companies to communicate electronically with their members. The annual report and accounts can now either be sent by e-mail or the information can be made available on a web site and the shareholders informed by any agreed means. Many large company now simply send shareholders and abbreviated version of the full report.

From the point of view of the major company, this offers an opportunity for cost savings on printing and postage. An e-mail sent to all or the majority of shareholders is a comparatively cheap way to comply with their legal obligation to provide annual accounts. The most obvious implication of this is that the glossy brochure containing the annual report and accounts will no longer be sent as a matter of course to all members.

But the reason that the annual report has become more and more concerned with glamour and spin is that it is also used as a promotional tool and that benefit is now going to be lost.

Arguably, the attempt to make the annual report more interesting to shareholders by the inclusion of additional information has resulted in the accounting requirements being relegated to the back of the booklet. Perhaps the annual accounts have become submerged within the promotional document.

As the use of the web to publish documents has developed, it has become very common indeed for companies to use PDF (portable document format) files as a way of making their reports available. This format allows readers to view the document precisely as it occurs in its original printed form, and circumvents an earlier objection to the use of the web in this context that it might lead to certain parts of a document being ignored. This is now no more likely than it would be in a conventional, printed annual report. PDF files also have the advantage of being highly secure.

One issue does need to be addressed. This is that making documents available on the web means that they are available to all-comers around the world. This has advantages for companies in that their information is easily available to larger number of investors and potential investors. But it has also increased the pressure for a humanization of international accounting standards, a topic that will be covered in a later part of this book.

SHARING INSIGHTS AND INFORMATION

A group of senior human resources managers and directors recently were debating how they could pass information such as new insights around their organizations. Indeed one, the manager of a training academy in a major telecommunications company, expressed the view that the biggest problem, or opportunity, facing them was how to pass learning from the engineers and others working on one project to the people tackling a similar project later on.

The e-dimension here is obvious, in that information recorded on the company intranet is available instantly to other people around the world. So, the technology is here. That just leaves the problem of motivating the people with the insights to share them – a much more difficult obstacle to overcome.

The e-dimension relates to annual reports in three ways.

» Comparing your organization's performance with the competition.
  Easy access to your competitors' annual reports gives you the opportunity to compare their strategy with yours, and, if you use the consistent model detailed in Chapter 10 of this book to do the analysis, also to compare financial performance and health. You can

in this way produce a very useful industry average by adding the results together and creating the average. This in turn allows you to see if the differences in financial performance give you any clues towards improvement.

» Building a picture of the critical success factors and comparative strengths of your customers.

In a similar way you can do the same thing for your customers. Indeed, if you are in a business that requires the selling process to involve understanding your customers' business and proposing solutions, then this is a *sine qua non*. Do the industry average as well as the individual and you will produce an interesting topic of conversation to discuss at top level.

» Checking the viability of suppliers.

Access to information on your suppliers, or perhaps more importantly prospective suppliers, could avoid the risk that you will do business with a company whose finances are thin or whose strategy is unlikely to maintain a competitive edge into the long term.

AN E-BASED KNOWLEDGE CENTRE

There are five main components of an e-based knowledge centre. Some of them are useful as concerns understanding accounts and some less so (sometimes called a company intranet).

Tools

The model this book proposes as the method of analyzing a company report can be a template included in an intranet. This means that teams can use a consistent methodology and a common business or financial language to improve productivity and communication. The understanding accounts tool has its place in this, as members of teams build a picture of the strategies and finances of organizations of interest to them.

E-learning

The availability of best-practice concepts and explanations, including, for example, understanding accounts, allows people with access to the knowledge centre to use a self-paced learning environment and "learning at the point of doing."

Experts

If, in trying to come to terms with an annual report, you need help, either with the process or the interpretation, an intranet gives you the names of and access to internal experts in your organization. This facility may include direct contact with the expert or the storage of frequently asked questions and insights.

Forum

Picking up the theme from the human resources director's cry for help, the forum becomes an important part of the intranet. Here like-minded individuals can discuss the analysis of their own or other organizations' reports. It is useful too in an environment where widespread teams are working on the same customers. For example, a person about to make contact with the Australian subsidiary of an American company can check with the knowledge base (see below) for an analysis of the report of the target company, prior to joining the forum set up to disseminate information about the global company.

Knowledge base

Building a knowledge base available worldwide depends on a growing series of real-life projects and cases being made available in a database. Taking the narrow example of understanding accounts, the availability and storage in the knowledge base of strategic and financial analysis of organizations that are key to your own is a very useful resource. On a wider basis, using consistent tools in many aspects of business processes builds the huge database of knowledge that the organization needs to maintain. They say we live in the information age; the problem is to keep information already generated in your organization, and prosper from it. Building real-life cases, with a consistent index for searching purposes, is the way that organizations will eventually solve this problem.

KEY LEARNING POINTS

The e-dimension impacts on the annual report in a number of ways. Companies will use it as a cheaper alternative to distributing the report. This makes a whole raft of information available to interested businesspersons. With the use of tools and other aspects of an intranet, Internet and intranet offer a further opportunity (or challenge if they don't take them up soon) for companies to make much better use of an important resource – the knowledge and experience of their people.

The Global Dimension

The global strategy that a company is pursuing is important to an observer of that company. This chapter shows how to use the annual report to find out what that strategy is, by:

» looking for the organizational aspects of globalization, and the balance of centralized/decentralized control;
» promulgating international standards for reporting.

"We are not a global business. We are a collection of local businesses with intense global coordination."
Percy Barnevik (b. 1941), former head of Asea Brown Boveri
(ABB)

Barnevik's neat summation of what a global business has to be helps us to understand what we need to look for in testing an annual report for the company's ability to survive and prosper on a global basis. The fashion for seeking global branding continues into this millennium, but it is now tempered by the realization that altering names, packaging, and advertising so that your product has the same appearance all over the world is not the whole solution.

In addition to the branding issue, cultural issues predominate. Francis Fukuyama, an American academic, summed this up as well as anyone: "International life will be seen increasingly as a competition not between rival ideologies – since most economically successful states will be organized along similar lines – but between different cultures."

Most individual managers learn about this the hard way. When one of the authors of this book first went to sell British products in the USA, he started off with an approach that could be summed up as "Unlike my European customers, US executives that I have to deal with predominantly speak English. I will therefore treat them as English people with a funny accent." How wrong could he be?

People experienced in doing business in Europe have a steep learning curve if they are to be successful in the USA and vice versa. Taking a simple example (and a sweeping generalization), there is a huge difference between how Americans and Europeans treat salespeople. In Europe the starting point of a sales prospect is a sort of growling suspicion, and the salesperson has to work hard to break this down and get the prospect in the first place to neutrality, before moving on to try to make them warm to the sales proposition. In America the attitude is much more welcoming and positive. They will congratulate you on the concept of your product and find as many positive things to say about it as they can. If, however, they actually see no need for it, or are aware of a competitive product they believe to be superior, the salesperson can end up with a totally wrong impression of the seriousness that the American prospect will bring to a consideration of the proposition.

Many salespeople from the UK have returned home from prospecting visits to North America promising stupendous orders that never in the end appear.

Now look at it from the opposite point of view. If an American executive gets into an aeroplane and travels from coast to coast, they will be in the aircraft for over five hours. They get out, and find much the same culture as the one they left behind. The same federal laws apply, the education system is very similar and, of course, their native tongue will do nicely. Now put the same American on to a flight from London to Paris, a 45-minute trip, and at the end of it they find themselves on what seems to be a different planet. They are much less used than Europeans are to adapting to different cultures.

Now expand your global thinking to include Japan, and the size of the cultural problem becomes massive. Even people who have worked in Japan and with Japanese people for some time still find it difficult to express how Japanese businesspeople operate.

We are trying to get from the annual report a view on the company's strategy and its capability in management terms and in financial terms to make it happen. So the question the annual report needs to answer is how well is a company dealing with the cultural or people side of globalization as well as the branding and marketing point of view?

THE STRATEGY FOR GLOBALIZATION

You will get some clues from the chairman's and directors' statements as to their attitude to this phenomenon. Look for the way the company is structured. The key is to look for control without standardization, plus the necessary standardization without the imposition of ways of working which are alien to far-flung cultures. If a head office insists on a standard that the local operations do not like, they will simply ignore it. The central initiative will fail.

A good detailed example of this is to look at how training is organized. This is not always given in great detail, but there is normally a clue as to whether the central powers are making different cultures use the same training process, which is also a strategy with a high probability of failure.

Look for how many layers there are between the group board and the operating companies. In the past, many US companies had a European head office. Often these were in Geneva or in London, particularly if London had been the company's springboard into Europe. The impact of this was in many cases matrix management. In a matrix management organization a human resources manager, for example, in a geographic region would have a boss in their own country and a dotted line to a human resources functional manager in Geneva. Head office managers wanted to look for best practices in one country and replicate them in another – not a bad idea if it made sense culturally. Typically what happened in such circumstances was that the European head office grew, and once it grew it started to have its own initiatives. So now rather than demonstrating the strengths of one operation and helping others to learn from it, head office has moved into laying down the law. Going back into the 1980s and 1990s there are legions of examples of that happening.

In the computing industry, for example, Geneva was home to people from all over Europe and America devising Europe-wide strategies and spending large budgets in trying to implement them. It is interesting to remember that when any downturn came, European head office was always an early and prime candidate for downsizing, and no one in the sharp end of country operating companies seemed to notice they had gone. Certainly no one I knew ever mourned their passing.

You will also find examples of how a company has carried out a restructuring of its international operations. If the report concentrates on the cost savings made from the restructuring, you may feel less comfortable that there has been a cultural consideration than if the report talks of consultation and international task forces. Are there any foreign members of the board, and how many of the overseas subsidiaries are managed by locals rather than expatriates from the company's country of origin?

THE FINANCES OF GLOBALIZATION

The other main implication for globalization and understanding an annual report concerns getting into a position where you are comparing apples with apples. Until relatively recently, each country followed its own accounting standards or followed the standards set by one of the major bodies, such as the Financial Accounting Standards Board (FASB) in the USA. Some global companies, particularly those from smaller countries such as the Scandinavian countries, of their own volition would print two versions of their results, one following their local standards and another following the US pattern.

In the USA, each state has its own corporations act and these do not contain detailed accounting regulations. Regulation of financial reporting in the USA is delegated to the Securities and Exchange Commission set up in the 1930s. Even then, this body has, in most instances, limited itself to a supervisory role and has looked to the accountancy profession for detailed standards. The FASB through its Statements of Financial Accounting Standards (SFASs) has laid down the detailed accounting rules – and detailed they are. The FASB is renowned for the quantity and thoroughness of its standards.

By contrast, in the UK accounting requirements have been included in the Companies Acts for over 50 years and the standard setters (currently the Accounting Standards Board – ASB) have been there to fill the gaps. This has led to many fewer standards than in the USA. Also, throughout the 1990s the then chairman of the ASB, Sir David Tweedie, was concerned to make standards deal with principles rather than providing a detailed cookbook.

Previously, international companies with a listing in the USA would prepare accounts following their local standards and provide a reconciliation to the standards laid down by FASB. In other situations companies prepared full accounts on the basis of both national standards and international standards.

The International Accounting Standards Committee (IASC) has existed since the 1970s but it is only in the last few years that International Accounting Standards (IASs) have taken on more prominence. Apart from the need to have international standards to deal with the rising number of global companies, IASs have now been fully recognized and are in the process of being fully implemented.

The International Accounting Standards Board (IASB) – part of the IASC – has since assumed responsibility for the implementation of international accounting standards and has built alliances with standard setting bodies around the world, with the result that IASC standards have now been adopted in 100 countries. In addition, standard setting bodies in the USA (see below) have moved decisively to adopt standards that are directly compatible with those of the IASB.

A list of accounting standards promulgated by the IASB is listed below:

IAS 1: Presentation of Financial Statements
IAS 2: Inventories
IAS 7: Cash Flow Statements
IAS 10: Events After the Balance Sheet Date
IAS 11: Construction Contracts
IAS 12: Income Taxes
IAS 14: Segment Reporting
IAS 15: Information Reflecting the Effects of Changing Prices
IAS 16: Property, Plant and Equipment
IAS 17: Leases
IAS 18: Revenue
IAS 19: Employee Benefits
IAS 20: Accounting for Government Grants and Disclosure of Government Assistance
IAS 21: The Effects of Changes in Foreign Exchange Rates
IAS 22: Business Combinations
IAS 23: Borrowing Costs
IAS 24: Related Party Disclosures
IAS 26: Accounting and Reporting by Retirement Benefit Plans
IAS 27: Consolidated Financial Statements
IAS 28: Investments in Associates
IAS 29: Financial Reporting in Hyperinflationary Economies
IAS 30: Disclosures in the Financial Statements of Banks and Similar Financial Institutions
IAS 31: Financial Reporting of Interests in Joint Ventures
IAS 32: Financial Instruments: Disclosure and Presentation
IAS 33: Earnings per Share
IAS 34: Interim Financial Reporting
IAS 35: Discontinuing Operations
IAS 36: Impairment of Assets
IAS 37: Provisions, Contingent Liabilities and Contingent Assets
IAS 38: Intangible Assets
IAS 39: Financial Instruments: Recognition and Measurement

IAS 40: Investment Property
IAS 41: Agriculture

Meanwhile, the international scene is characterized by more and more cooperation. New issues are now debated internationally and a joint approach is often agreed before new draft standards are exposed for comment. The same Sir David Tweedie who previously led the UK's standard setting body chairs the new board setting international standards. This should help standardization with the UK approach.

But the real key to the future is the reaction from the USA. Will IASs be seen as detailed enough to deal with all of the issues previously covered by the FASB? Will the USA give up its own standard setting role? In February 2000, the SEC asked whether foreign companies issuing accounts in the USA should be allowed to do so based purely on IASs without a reconciliation to US standards. There was widespread support from around the world for the suggestion, although not surprisingly there was opposition from FASB and some in the accountancy profession. The thing that is interesting is that the question is being asked at all. Writing in *Accountancy* magazine in November 2000, David Damant, a board member of the IASC, said "As for the US, the American authorities' commitment to the IASC's new structure is so complete as to indicate that US GAAP (Generally accepted accounting practice) and IASs look likely to converge in a relatively short timescale."

This remark appears to have been remarkably prescient as the IASB, on behalf of the IASC and US standards setters signed a memorandum of understanding in 2002 and moreover, are now co-operating fully and recognize the need for US and international standards to be closely linked. Full convergence will take time, but both bodies are working in this direction, and the move has also been endorsed by the US Securities & Exchange Commission.

The IASB is now moving to harmonize reporting standards for companies, and has issued a number of IFRS (international financial reporting standards) statements, to which public companies around the world are expected to adhere. These are in the process of being implemented to the end that all companies should be reporting fully on IAS/IFRS bases by the latter part of 2006.

The moves to harmonize international standards of accounting and reporting have brought the predictable objections for companies and from analysts. Most complain that they introduce additional complexity and volatility into financial statements by requiring companies, for example, to treat share options granted to employees as remuneration, to reflect changes in the value of pension fund assets and liabilities on the face of the profit and loss account, and to value derivatives contracts used for hedging in the same way.

The simplest way of countering these objections is to point out that the increased complexity of financial statements is that it is no more or less than ensuring they reflect accurately the increased complexity of the underlying businesses themselves. Investors should welcome this, since it makes events like the examples of Polly Peck and Enron less likely to occur in the future.

KEY LEARNING POINTS

Most medium sized and all large companies have a global dimension. You can make progress detecting their approach to this from the text of the annual report. Look for attention to the cultural aspects of globalization as well as for standardization and centralization. Remember the quote that opened this chapter.

In terms of the financial part of the report, the authorities are working hard on global standards and should ensure that people reading an annual report from whatever source are looking at a consistent set of figures.

06

The State of the Art

This chapter considers how to use detective work on the data available in the annual report to understand the past. It looks at:

» the general business model – finance;
» details of the main financial statements;
» the starting point for understanding the past.

"One of our most important management tasks is maintaining the proper balance between short-term profit growth and investment for future strength and growth."

David Packard (1912-96), founder of Hewlett-Packard
computer company

THE FINANCIAL STATEMENTS

As the business environment changes, financial reporting also changes to meet new demands. What ratios and measures analysts and finance directors use come into fashion and go out again. However, the underlying basics of reading the financial pages have stood the test of time.

The art of understanding the financial section of an annual report has four components, all of which we will discuss in this chapter; but first of all we need to agree a general model for tracing the progress of cash around a business. From the loan capital and share capital put up to start the enterprise off, round the working capital cycle. Then we need to identify the three main financial reports that we will use – the profit and loss account, the balance sheet, and the cash flow statement. We will look at the contents of all three. Finally we will take the first look at the ratios that we can derive from these reports, commenting on their usefulness.

This is the nuts and bolts of understanding the financial statements; you can then progress to their main uses in Chapter 7 "In Practice".

THE GENERAL BUSINESS MODEL

To understand business finance it is useful to have a diagrammatic illustration of how money flows round a business – see Fig. 6.1.

The capital employed in the business comes from shareholders and lenders. The undistributed part of a company's earnings stays in the business and belongs to the shareholders. Retained profits, in most cases, increase shareholders' funds on an annual basis.

This capital goes into the company as cash – the first step in the working capital cycle. Managers spend this cash on, for example, raw materials, labor, and overheads in the case of a manufacturer, or mainly

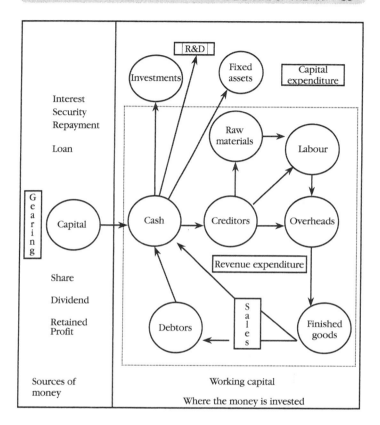

Fig. 6.1 The general business model.

on labor in a service business. Production thus produces a stock of finished goods which are sold to customers for either cash or credit. In a service industry there is no stock, although there may be, in slow times, idle labor. Labor is not the same as stock, of course, because you can store stock for the future, idle time is labor lost. If a service industry, such as a recruitment firm, has the right number of executives in good times, unfortunately it may have to get rid of some of them in bad times.

Also in the working capital cycle are creditors. These are present when materials or services which this company acquires from others are supplied on credit.

Here's an example of an industry which, because of the nature of its business, can excel in speeding cash round its working capital cycle. From a recent set of accounts of a major food supermarket, we can see that it takes less than 20 days from when it receives goods until the sales proceeds are in its bank account. Customers pay on the spot with cash or a card. With a payment period to its creditors of about 25 days, you find that all its working capital needs are funded by its creditors.

It's not so easy when you are selling complex products to customers with time to study and compare before spending large sums of money.

In the same period a leading aerospace manufacturer holds its inventory for over 100 days before it even starts to collect its money from its customers.

So, from these physical examples we can see that ideally raw materials and parts will be incorporated into the product on the day they are delivered by the supplier. In this ideal world someone will buy each product as it comes off the assembly line rather than into stock or inventory. And finally in this commercial Utopia customers will pay their bills on the day the product is delivered.

In fact the world is not the ideal one described above and it takes considerable organizational effort just to make businesses as efficient as their competitors, and even more to achieve some sort of advantage to give them competitive edge. Expenditure on items within the working capital cycle is known as revenue expenditure, since its purpose is to create the revenue or income of the business. Revenue expense is an immediate cost which reduces the profits of the enterprise.

Managers can use the cash generated by a business for the long-term development of the business. Long-term investments are in fixed assets and research and development. A company can also invest cash in other companies – buying some or all of their shares. The full cost of capital expenditure is not normally taken off the profits of the year the investment is made but is spread over time. This is known as depreciation. Keep the general business model in your head as a simple template. We are going to add some complications, but none that invalidate this picture.

On a regular basis the finance department of the enterprise, whether internal or external, reports to the shareholders on progress during the preceding period. It issues reports at the half-year stage or on a quarterly basis, but the biggest interest and publicity is given to the annual report. The next part of this chapter deals with the main financial statements – the profit and loss account, the balance sheet, and the cash flow statement – which companies use to control their businesses and report to their owners.

Most managers are familiar with the profit and loss account. Indeed most normal people understand the concept of comparing what you are earning with what you are spending. Let's explain the document and comment on each of the items.

Often called the earnings statement, the profit and loss account covers a period of time. In the case of most large companies, they publish this statement twice a year. During the third quarter of the year they publish a profit and loss account that covers the first half of the year including comparisons with the first half of last year. During the first quarter of the next year they publish the full year's figures.

THE PROFIT AND LOSS ACCOUNT

The profit and loss account compares the sales revenue earned during a period with the costs incurred in making those sales. The figures are based on the accruals concept. That is, revenue is included for all goods dispatched, whether or not payment has been received by the end of the period. Similarly, cost will include the cost of all goods and services received before the end of the period. They may not have been paid for, or even invoiced, at the balance sheet date, but their cost is still included.

Here is an outline of the statement together with some explanation – remember there is also the glossary section in Chapter 8, and more detailed definitions in Chapter 10.

The top line of a profit and loss account is the sales made, as you can see from Fig. 6.2. These are sometimes called "revenues" or "net revenues." Other companies use the term *sales turnover*. Be careful, "turnover" has a different meaning in the USA where it is normally reserved for "staff turnover."

The Profit and Loss Account

Sales
minus Cost of Sales

=Gross profit

minus selling and distribution expenses
minus administrative overheads

=Trading profit (earnings before interest and tax)

minus interest

=Net profit before tax

minus tax

=Profit attributable to shareholders

minus dividends

=Retained profit

Fig. 6.2   The profit and loss account.

From this we deduct the actual costs of the products sold. In the simple case of a bookshop, for example, it is what is paid for each of the books sold. In a manufacturing company it includes all the direct costs of producing the products sold. The jargon term usually used is *cost of sales*. A lot of managers also call these costs "direct costs."

This gives us the *gross profit*. From the gross profit we can calculate the gross margin. This is a vital piece of information for monitoring purposes. How we run the business is dictated to a considerable extent by how big our gross margins are.

In fact, one of the most important characteristics of a business is its gross margin, or rather gross margins, since most companies sell a range of products and services which will probably have different margins. The gross margin of a product is the gross profit expressed as a percentage of the sales proceeds. In most cases there is a good reason for the margins that companies can achieve. For example, if there is a high level of after-sales support required, then plainly the gross margin will have to be high. The costs of after-sales service and support come out of the gross profit. When any businessperson looks at the characteristics of a business, the gross margin is an important starting point.

From the gross margin we deduct the expenses. For annual reporting purposes they are divided into *selling and distribution expenses* and *administrative overheads*. It is fairly straightforward to know which is which. The costs of most of head office, for example, will go into overheads, while the costs of running the fleet of delivery vans will be part of selling and distribution expenses. In some businesses this is a crucial distinction, and some of the ratios in this area will be significant, but normally it is less important to distinguish between the two. We do not intend to pay too much attention to it.

This gives us the *trading profit* or earnings. This is often described as earnings before interest and tax, or EBIT. Now reduce this by *interest* and you get the number for the *net profit before tax*. There is no golden rule, but this is generally the figure which people talk about when they are making comparisons. In the business papers, when it says "the profits are down" it is probably referring to this number on the profit and loss account.

The board then makes a provision out of profits to pay its corporate taxes, and may pay a dividend out of the remainder before finally crediting to the shareholders the portion which is kept in the business. The *retained profit* is the item which connects the profit and loss account to the balance sheet, as we will see.

THE BALANCE SHEET

The balance sheet is a more difficult concept for most people to understand than the profit and loss account, but the two statements together give much better clues to the health and prospects of a company than the earnings statement on its own. Indeed, at the top of a business there will be much more emphasis placed on understanding the impact of events on the balance sheet, while middle managers are more concerned with the shorter term profit position.

One of the differences between the two documents is that a profit and loss account shows what happened over a period of time, while a balance sheet is a snapshot of the company's position at a moment in time. This moment could be any day in the financial year, but the one we are most familiar with is the balance sheet produced at the end of the company year and published with the report.

The two sides of a balance sheet, the assets and liabilities, are generally shown one on top of the other. The name of the document comes from the fact that the total of these two concepts must equal each other. All the assets the company has must be matched in aggregate by some form of borrowing, share capital, reserve or provision. Let's take it step by step. Figures 6.3 and 6.4 show the most common layouts for a US and a UK balance sheet, respectively.

It may be difficult to believe, but the different terms used refer to exactly the same things. So "accounts receivable" (US) is the same as "debtors" (UK), and so on. Once again, let's explain each item.

What the company owns are called *assets*, and what the business owes are called *liabilities*.

We group the assets by time considerations. *Current assets* are those which we are likely to turn into cash within the next 12 months.

» *Stock* (called "inventory" in the USA) is the stock of finished goods not yet sold or delivered. A manufacturer also includes work in progress and raw materials in its stock.
» *Debtors* are mainly the amounts customers owe for unpaid invoices.
» *Cash* is the most liquid asset of all.

Assets which will give benefit over a longer term are called *fixed assets*. These are subdivided into *tangible* and *intangible*

» The tangible assets in a shop, for example, are the *furnishings and fittings*. In a factory there is *plant and machinery*, and so on. Don't forget that the cost of these assets are charged to the profit and loss account using the mechanism known as depreciation.

Land and property, also tangible fixed assets, can be different, since they are liable to appreciate in value. We may record that appreciation from time to time based on an independent valuation.

The balance sheet (US)

Assets

Current assets
      Cash
      Accounts receivable
      Inventory

Fixed assets
      Tangible
      Intangible
      Long term investments

Liabilities and shareholders' equity

Current liabilities
      Short term borrowings
      Accounts payable

Long term debt

Other liabilities

Shareholders' equity
      Issued stock
      Retained earnings

Fig. 6.3 The balance sheet (US).

» Intangible assets are getting less common on balance sheets. There is a healthy suspicion of assets which are said to have a value but no substance. A key element of intangible assets is *goodwill*, which is the extra amount the company has paid for an acquisition over and above the value of its assets. The other common type of fixed asset is *trade investments*. These are investments in other companies which the board expects to be holding for the long term.

```
Assets
Fixed assets
        Tangible
        Intangible
        Investments
Current assets
        Stock
        Debtors
        Cash in bank and at hand
Creditors: Amounts falling due within one year
Creditors: Amounts falling due after more than one year
Provisions for liabilities and charges
Capital and reserves
        Called up share capital
        Share premium account
        Reserves
        Profit and loss account
```

Fig. 6.4 The balance sheet (UK).

Now let us turn to liabilities. Once again the same definition occurs. Current liabilities are those liabilities which we will have to pay within the next 12 months. It is a strict definition.

In this category we include:

» the *overdraft* which the bank can recall at any time;
» any *short term loans* which will have to be repaid within the next year;
» *creditors* accounts payable, including the most important item trade creditors, which are bills from suppliers the company still has to pay;
» a *dividend* that has been announced but not yet paid; and
» *tax* – a common item which we need to pay within 12 months.

So much for current liabilities. Long-term liabilities are also known as fixed liabilities. We can group them into long-term external liabilities, and liabilities to the shareholders.

External liabilities include: *long-term loans* and *provisions for liabilities and charges*. Most balance sheets have an element of the latter, which are liabilities that will probably have to be paid at some time but not within a year. The most common example is deferred taxation. Another example would be liabilities arising out of a legal obligation to decontaminate a site.

That just leaves shareholders' funds and minority interests.

Shareholders' funds normally have the following three elements.

» *Share capital*, which is the nominal value of the issued shares. Most UK shares are valued at a nominal 25 pence, most US shares have a par value of $1. If, however, the board were to issue more shares to raise capital, it would sell them at somewhere near the current market value. The difference between those numbers is recorded as *share premium*. The Americans, slightly more plainly, call it "moneys paid above par."

» The *reserves*, mostly accumulated retained profits, as we have seen, also belong to the shareholders. They build up over time, and companies which have traded for a long time will have a lot of money in reserves. One item which must be shown separately is the "profit and loss account", which is the total of past retained profits. Other reserves you might come across include the revaluation reserve, which arises when assets are revalued.

» The final item is *minority interests*. This figure is similar to reserves. It records what part of the reserves belong to minority interests, that is profits which have been made by companies within the group which have other shareholders apart from the parent company which is presenting the report.

Once again, the terminology will change according to the situation and the norms agreed by the finance director.

THE CASHFLOW STATEMENT

All managers look after the profit and loss account, smart managers understand the importance of the good management of cash flow. Ask any self-employed person and they will tell you that cash flow is what it is all about. It is harder to recognize this fact when you work for a large concern because, in most cases, others look after cash flow. It can seem to the people in the middle that there is an unlimited pot of cash to spend out there, and that a megacorp is always going to be able to spend up to its budgets.

In small companies the cash flow is a frequent (even daily) calculation as the firm tries to expand without running out of cash. But even in a large company the cash position is an important issue in its ability to achieve its strategy.

Well-run companies make everyone aware of cash flow or set targets, such as how quickly managers have to get their customer invoices paid, which eventually end up assisting the company with its cash flow. Companies do not necessarily go bust because they are not making profits, they go out of business, or get taken over, because they do not have the cash to pay their bills.

The cash situation of a company can be dramatically different from its profit situation. For example, a company making good net profit before tax, may have a problem if its cash flow is insufficient to repay loan capital at the appropriate time. Remember too that it is essential for a chairman who is going to carry out his or her promises on dividend to have the cash in hand to pay the amounts expected.

For middle managers the cash flow statement in the annual report is probably less important than the information they get in management accounts concerning cash, but we need to take a quick look.

Using fairly typical terms, the cash flow statement in an annual report looks like Fig. 6.5.

» *Net cash flow from operating activities.* The statement itself starts from the net cash flow from operating activities. You can normally tie this back to the profit and loss account, using the reconciliation in the notes to the accounts. One of the main differences between cash flow and profit relates to depreciation. Depreciation is simply a notional book entry, an amount set aside from profits each year to cover the eventual cost of replacing fixed assets in the balance sheet. It does not involve any cash flowing out of the business, until these assets are eventually replaced. As a result it is added back to arrive at cash flow.

» *Returns on investment and servicing of finance.* You are then told how much was paid and received in the servicing of finance - the interest paid and received.

» *Taxation.* Now comes the next cash item, tax paid. Remember that this will probably be different from the amount of tax provided

Net cash inflow from operating activities
Returns on investment and servicing of finance
Taxation
Capital investment and financial investment
Acquisitions and disposals
Equity dividends paid
Management of liquid resources
Financing
Increase/decrease in cash in the period
Reconciliation of net cash flow to movement in net debt

Fig. 6.5   The cash flow statement.

against profits. Tax on this year's profits may not be paid until next year.

» *Capital expenditure and financial investment.* This covers investment and disposal of fixed assets and trade investments.

» *Acquisitions and disposals.* Where a company has taken over or sold the whole or a major part of a business, it shows the cash implication of that here. Later in the notes you get the detail of the balance sheet items which were bought or sold. Obviously this has an impact on the group balance sheet at the end of the year and could be very important in the case of a company which has a declared strategy of acquisition. Cash outflows are shown in brackets.

» *Equity dividends paid.* This is the sum of dividends paid to shareholders. There is usually a difference between the figure near the foot of the profit and loss account and this number. This is because the cash flow statement shows the dividends actually paid during the year, which will include the previous year's final proposed dividend, but exclude the current proposed dividend which will be paid out during the following year. The profit and loss account records the dividends related to the current year profits irrespective of whether they have been paid.

We could have made the same point earlier with respect to interest paid and received, tax paid, and capital expenditure. In every case the cash flow statement records the actual amount paid or received, whereas the profit and loss account records the amounts payable or receivable.

» *Financing*. This records the change in capital employed.

» *Increase/decrease in cash in the period*. This is the bottom line of the cash flow.

» *Reconciliation of net cash flow to movement in net debt*. This section explains in detail changes in net debt. This information, which is mandatory in the UK, helps to link the cash flow to the balance sheet.

In conclusion, the cash flow statement gives an indication of the relationship between profitability and the ability to generate cash. As we have seen, profits without cash lead to ruin. Analysts will often develop models to assess the value of a company by reference to the present value of its future cash flows. The historical cash flow statement is useful in two ways. First, analysts will be able to use cash information rather than just profit information in their models. Second, they will be able to use the historical cash flow to check the accuracy of previous predictions.

UNDERSTANDING THE PAST

We now deal with the financial ratios which people use at corporate level to compare last year with this year, and one business with another. So that we quickly get to the relevance and usefulness of such ratios, we will start with an overview of how four of the ratios offer the opportunity to get an impression of the financial status of a company. Following this, we will look at a benchmark or pattern for a company going through a 30-year life cycle. We will see how the ratios change with time, and how the different stages of development appeal to different sets of investors.

An overview of four key ratios

These key corporate ratios are revealed in the annual report and talked about in the financial pages.

Senior managers are mainly interested in these ratios because they have a part in setting the share price, driving the strategy of the business, and, of course, driving the financial part of the business plan. If a middle manager is asked to take an objective concerning profit margin, it is wise to know how such a ratio is calculated.

Company reports are notorious, of course, for what they hide as well as what they reveal. It is possible, at least in the short term, for creative accountants and their boardroom masters to produce numbers that reflect more accurately their aspirations for the company than its actual performance. However, this does tend to disappear with time. As the business continues to perform in a certain way, so the accountants will eventually force the board to break bad news to its shareholders.

Despite this caveat, the annual report does give some very useable information. The most useful of the ratios are *capital gearing*, *income gearing*, *return on capital employed*, and the *pretax profit margin*.

Armed with these four ratios you can start to understand the pressures on the board, and through them the pressures on the managers of the business.

The key financial ratios

The four ratios below give an effective check on progress quite quickly. They are reasonably easy to calculate, and with practice take a matter of a few minutes to produce. Always do them for the two years in the report, or even for four or five years, so you can get a feel for how they have changed. You can then check the directors' statements to see if they comment on changes that you regard as significant.

Frequently, the report will include "facts for shareholders" or "five-year record" that include some calculated ratios. The advantage of these is that they remove the need to do any calculations. Unfortunately there are two disadvantages to relying on these that make them much less useful than calculating them yourself.

The first problem is that the published ratios are calculated in a way that suits each company. They will use figures that, while they are not misleading or inaccurate, give a gloss on performance, which the truly objective investigator wishes to avoid.

The second problem is connected. Companies use ratios that suit themselves and therefore do not use the same ones as others. So for the sake of consistency it is better to become very familiar with four ratios you work out for yourself.

You can also build a personal database of examples giving you various benchmarks for examining and comparing any company. This is particularly true if you study only one or a limited number of business sectors.

One final point of introduction. The rules of thumb quoted below are useful as you learn to appreciate the significance of the ratios. They are guides only, however, and their significance varies depending on the business the company is in and the stage in its life cycle it has reached.

Capital gearing

This ratio compares a company's debt with total capital employed – the sum of shareholders' funds and debt. Shareholders' funds, or equity, include the money that the investors originally put into the company plus the profits which have been retained over the years. The debt involved here is the money owing on a long-term basis to banks and other financial institutions. Some analysts simply compare debt to equity, perhaps a more logical approach to capital gearing.

High gearing, where there is a lot of debt compared to shareholders' funds, involves using other people's money to make money for yourself. In fact, most of us in our private lives have one high-geared transaction from which, over time, we generally make a good profit. We own a house with a mortgage. Suppose you buy a house for £130,000 with capital of £26,000 and a mortgage of £104,000. This gives the relatively high gearing of 80% debt and 20% equity. If the housing market does well, you may well find yourself in 10 years time living in a house worth £260,000, or double what you paid. The equity you have in it increases by considerably more than double, even assuming you have made no repayments of capital. Your equity has gone up from £26,000 to £156,000, a six-fold increase. This is the positive side of gearing.

The downside of gearing is that you have to make regular interest payments and probably put some money aside each month to enable you to repay the mortgage at some time in the future.

The other downside is that just as your gain was exaggerated by gearing, so is any loss. If, as has happened in most housing markets, there is a decline in prices over a number of years, then you lose. Take a decrease in value of 20%, or £26,000 in your case, and you have lost all your money. Worse than that and you hit so-called negative equity, where the loan is higher than the value of the asset.

It is much like this in a business. Run at low gearing and you miss the opportunity to make money for yourself while using other people's capital, or run at high gearing and run the risk of profits lowered by interest charges and a cash flow strapped by repayment commitments.

RULE OF THUMB – CAPITAL GEARING

Using the very simple ratio of long-term debt as a percentage of shareholders' funds plus long-term debt:

» low gearing is less than 10%;
» medium gearing is about 33%; and
» high gearing is about 66% or over.

Income gearing

Income gearing tests the ability of a company to pay its interest bill out of its profits. It is calculated by expressing interest payable as a percentage of earnings before interest and tax. Some analysts turn this on its head and use the concept of 'interest cover, which is found by dividing profit before interest and tax by interest. Looking at the positive side of income gearing you see the leveraging affect on profit again. Take the case of a company with income gearing of 60%, as shown in Table 6.1.

Table 6.1   Income gearing of 60%.

Earnings before interest and tax	100
Interest payable	60
Profit for shareholders	40

See how the gearing affect exaggerates the effect of a modest rise or fall in profits. Table 6.2 shows the impact of earnings increasing or decreasing by 10%.

Table 6.2 Income gearing increasing or decreasing by 10%.

	10% Increase	10% Decrease
Earnings before interest and tax	110	90
Interest payable	60	60
Profit for shareholders	50	30

In both cases the 10% change in earnings has had a 25% impact on the profit available for shareholders. This is known as financial leverage.

RULE OF THUMB – INCOME GEARING

If you calculate the ratio as interest payable as a percentage of earnings before interest paid and tax:

» low gearing is less than 25%;
» medium gearing is between 26% and 75%; and
» high gearing is above 75%.

Return on capital employed (RoCE)

The next two ratios in this overview are two profitability ratios. The first compares a number from the profit and loss account, profits before tax, with those items on the balance sheet that make up the long-term capital used in the business. This long-term capital is made up of long-term liabilities, share capital and reserves.

RULE OF THUMB – RETURN ON CAPITAL EMPLOYED

Calculated as net profit before interest paid and tax divided by long-term capital:

» low profitability is from 0 to 10%;
» medium profitability is between 10% and 20%; and
» high profitability is above 20%.

Over time it tells us what we need to know about the health of the company measured by profits. After all, the reason people put money into companies is so that managers use it to make a return. If the managers cannot do it, then there are always bonds and banks that can.

Pretax profit margin

This is a profit and loss account ratio. It compares the bottom line of the profit and loss account with the top line, profits with sales. It tells how much profit was earned for each pound or dollar of sales. As we will see, it is not only a corporate measure, but it is also is one of the principal measures used when managers are running divisions and profit centers.

RULE OF THUMB – PRE-TAX PROFIT MARGIN

Calculated as net profit before tax as a percentage of sales revenues it looks like this:

» low margin is below 2%;
» medium margin is between 4% and 8%; and
» high margin is above 10%.

Remember that all measures, and particularly this one, are highly dependent on the industry you are looking at. What is a poor margin for technology companies, for example, could be a very good one for a bookshop.

KEY LEARNING POINTS

We have learnt how cash cycles round the general business model, and examined the contents of the three most frequently used financial statements – the profit and loss account, the balance sheet, and the cash flow statement. Finally we looked at four key ratios that you can calculate quickly to compare the performance of one company against a reasonable rule of thumb. We have to repeat the caveat that these rules of thumb may differ widely from industry sector to industry sector.

07

In Practice

How do you draw conclusions from reading the annual report? Does it enable you to predict the future. This chapter draws on the following examples to answer these questions:

» a comparison of Nokia with Ericsson;
» understanding Centrica;
» watching for a change in strategy – GEC/Marconi.

"The secret of success is to know something nobody else knows."
Aristotle Onassis (1906–1975), Greek-born ship owner

The structure of this chapter is as follows. First we look at another couple of ratios that help you put the report and accounts of a company into context. These are the two principal shareholder ratios – yield and price/earnings. This gives us the opportunity to look at a benchmark company at different stages in its development. Such a benchmark should make the last part of the chapter more useful.

In that part we will look at a number of companies with their financial ratios from the past. We will also note what happened next, and how much of that was predictable, on the balance of probabilities. This should give you good interpretative clues when you move to using the model for company reports that you wish to understand.

SHAREHOLDER RATIOS

In the annual report you will find reference to the main shareholder ratios, but in order to make the best interpretation of the figures you will need to use the most up to date information. You will find this in the business pages of any reasonable newspaper.

Yield

The yield of a share is a measure of the return on investment an investor receives in the form of dividend. This is a percentage and reflects the dividend return you can expect if you buy the shares at today's price and the company pays the same amount in dividend as it did last year.

For example, a sector that tends to have a high yield is the electricity sector. As a utility sector it is not seen as having huge opportunities for growth. But it is a pretty safe sector since even in difficult times in the business cycle everybody still puts the lights on and cooks food.

This means that people use this sector to get the relatively safe dividend income. This makes the dividend strategy generous. The share price is kept low by the perception of low growth potential in the industry. The combination of these two things gives the sector a high yield.

The opposite of this is the case in, for example, information technology, where dividends are kept relatively low to keep money in the business to fund growth and research, and the share price reflects the huge opportunities that the market thinks the sector has. These two factors give the sector a low yield.

This last point is the complicating factor. Unless they have other information from published or other sources, a new investor in a company will expect the managers to maintain or increase the annual dividend. They can only do this, of course, if the company has the profits and cash to do so. When a yield suddenly goes very high, it means that the share price has dropped significantly, and that often means that investors, that is the market, are unsure whether the dividend will be maintained either now or in the future.

Price/earnings ratio

The second shareholder ratio is the price/earnings (P/E) ratio. We can discuss the price/earnings ratio as

P/E = market capitalization/total earnings

Simply by dividing top and bottom of this expression by the number of shares in issue, we get the more common form of P/E ratio as

P/E = share price/earnings per share

This last expression, earnings per share, is a very important one in the vocabulary of shareholders and their chairman, as we shall see as we look at how companies present their reports.

LOOKING FOR A BENCHMARK

There is no such thing as a typical company. Its different products, markets, and management styles make each enterprise unique. It is, however, possible to use the history of a composite company, Compusell, as a benchmark of the characteristics and ratios of a company over a long period of time. Each of these snapshots represents a real company, but to make the benchmark work we have taken the fiction that it is the same company throughout, and given it a fictitious name. All the statements from the chairman come from actual annual reports.

THE 30-YEAR HISTORY OF COMPUSELL

Stage 1 – Inception to 7 years old

Turn back the clock to the time when large mainframe computers were under attack from smaller more flexible mini-computers. At that time an electronics engineer created Compusell. The newly floated company had, in the early stages, the ability to generate very rapid growth of sales. The market is eager for the new computer concept, and the co-owners, a venture capital company, are happy to put money into the new venture.

Compusell is very aggressive at this stage. It needs volume to cover its voracious appetite for cash as it invests millions of dollars in production infrastructure. This makes its competitiveness very sharp. It will, to a considerable extent, sacrifice profit for market share. It hires a salesforce of "hunters" – salespeople who enjoy the challenge of getting new business in fast. These salespeople are good at closing business and handling objections. If they do not close business fast, they go elsewhere. Most would say that it is easier to run a company enjoying high growth of sales. The problem is to keep a contingency plan in mind if the growth falters for even a short period of time. Look for such a plan in the report of a company at this stage of development.

We should expect to find high morale in the company as business markets flock to the upstart.

The annual report

In the chairman's report we will expect to see a reflection of this growth. The following extracts are from the chairman's statement for a stage 1 company:

"June saw another milestone when we shipped mini-computer number 100,000."

"Our sales growth last year exceeded 50%, and although this is likely to prove exceptional, Compusell is confident of its ability to take further advantage of the expanding market over the next few years."

The report's tone will reflect the excitement and enthusiasm of the fledgling discovering success for the first time.

The ratios

The board is running Compusell by its cash flows rather than by its profit and loss account. It needs huge amounts of cash for capital investment and we expect to find very high levels of borrowing. This high gearing will show itself in both of the gearing ratios; with a high percentage of debt and very little profit left over once interest is deducted.

Profitability will be relatively low measured by both return on capital employed and the profit margin.

COMPUSELL'S RATIOS AT STAGE 1

Gearing	75%
Income gearing	95%
RoCE	1%
Pretax profit margin	1%

The investors' ratios

Investors will find that the market only sees Compusell as having long-term potential in the high-risk part of their portfolios. It is undesirable for the company to pay large amounts in dividend, since it needs all its cash to fund its expansion. So the yield will be low, or no dividend will be paid at all.

The P/E will be very high as the market calculates future profit streams for the company as it gets into a position to exploit its assets. There is one other ratio to bring in here. Dividends are, as we have said, paid out of profit. It is useful to know what percentage of profit is needed to pay the dividend. The term we use is "dividend cover" – the number of times the dividend is covered by the profits. If there is little left over having paid the dividend, the company may be starved of money for growth or it may not be possible in the future to maintain the existing level of dividend. In this case, Compusell's dividend cover may very well be high, not because the profits are huge but because the dividend is stingy. In fact many high growth companies pay no dividends until they become well established.

COMPUSELL'S INVESTOR RATIOS AT STAGE 1

Yield	0.3%
Price/earnings	35
Dividend cover	13

Stage 2 – From 7 years to 15 years

Compusell has come of age. It has survived the heady days of 30% year on year growth and shown itself to be competitive. It has a viable market share in the areas where it already operates and is looking for new opportunities to make further investment either in new markets, such as overseas, or in new product areas, such as personal computers.

This diversified growth will still cost a lot of money, but the business now generates a healthy cash flow and is profitable. There is still a fair amount of risk in the company. It is vulnerable to making mistakes as it moves into new activities. No matter how good the prospects, it is always more risky to take old products into new markets, or new products into old markets, than to keep doing more of the same.

The annual report

We will expect now to see the chairman talking of some consolidation of its current affairs, although the emphasis of the report will still be on growth. Look for the new initiatives.

The following extracts are from the chairman's statement for a stage 2 company:

"Our earnings per share before exceptional items grew some 22%."

"Our strengthening financial position allows us to explore new countries seeking our products, whilst at the same time consolidating our strategy to focus on those parts of the world where we are already strong and where our returns will be the greatest."

The ratios

The debt ratios are still high. Almost certainly by this time the company will have been back to its investors for more cash through a rights issue. At this stage the venture capital shareholders will have taken some profits and reduced their holding. This, of course, radically reduces the debt to equity ratio, but it will rise again to reflect further borrowing to continue investment.

Profitability has improved to what could be described as fairly safe levels. This means that the current business will produce reliable profits, and it is only in the new areas of activity that there is still high risk.

COMPUSELL'S RATIOS AT STAGE 2

Gearing	60%
Income gearing	75%
RoCE	10%
Pretax profit margin	4%

The investors' ratios

Compusell wants to pay out some dividend of real worth. It probably had to make promises in this area when it made its last cash call to shareholders and it sees dividend as a sign of impending "respectability." Nevertheless, the yield is still well below the sector average, as the price of the share is buoyed by the market's expectation of further growth.

The P/E is also still very high. It is probably less than other new entrants in stage 1 of their life cycles, but it will be well above the industry average. The Compusell example is valid when you compare the relative measures of, for example, price/earnings. But the whole market fluctuates as well. So the rule of thumb has to be adjusted up or down depending on the general health of equities.

The dividend is stretching cover much more than in the first phase. Investors are starting to ask when the return on their money will start to come through, and there is no room for the very high dividend cover of the earlier stage.

COMPUSELL'S INVESTOR RATIOS AT STAGE 2

Yield	1.6%
Price/earnings	25
Dividend cover	3.5

Stage 3 – From 15 years to 23 years

The company has achieved respectability. It is now well into the Standards and Poor 500 companies – the top 500 industrials measured by market capitalization. It is a complex company and the analysts are looking for good statements of strategy proving that the current management can run a cruiser, having been very successful in managing fast patrol boats and destroyers.

At this stage the type of manager required to run the business is different from the original people who got it to this size. People who were at their best during the exciting start up and second phase may not be as competent in this bigger enterprise. Unless they can make the change they might be better to move on rather than become frustrated in an environment to which they are not entirely suited. We will probably see changes at board level for this reason.

Its share price varies with the changes in the industry. A bad regulatory change, particularly in software bundling, for example, could endanger profit growth significantly. Long-term planning is no longer a luxury, but a vital responsibility of the board and its advisers.

It has some "big names" on its board with an ex-senator amongst its numbers.

Risk has changed in its nature. The company could now afford to make some mistakes without threatening its actual life. The market sees the risk as comparable to other stocks in the sector. Investors see reports of sell-offs of one share in the sector and swaps into other companies in the same sector being recommended.

The annual report

It is unlikely that the annual report will claim that everything is rosy. Shareholders expect more circumspect statements with admissions of error and promises of remedy. A careful look at the ratios that the chairman chooses to report can be revealing. For example, if he produces a graph showing that the past 20 years of share price has consistently out-performed the market index, he is probably trying to reassure the market that there is still plenty of growth potential there. He does not want the growth in share price to stall, although it will certainly have slowed.

The following extracts are from the chairman's statement for a stage 3 company:

"We see alliances with other companies as an important contributor to our vision to be the supplier of choice for people seeking high levels of features combined with international coverage."

"New technologies offer enormous opportunities to broaden the products and services available to our current customers. The Internet will radically alter the way we conduct our lives."

"The reorganization which we completed during the year has ensured that we can carry through our promises of presenting a global image and relationship with our key accounts worldwide."

The ratios

The ratios have now reached the mature end of industry averages. Gearing is at the low risk end and less than one-third of profits are required to pay the interest bill.

The measure of return on capital employed is as meaningful and reliable as any other large company's, and reflects the sorts of return expected from the whole sector as opposed to the rapid growth part of the sector. The relatively high pretax profit margin shows the good profitability of the information technology sector.

COMPUSELL'S RATIOS AT STAGE 3

Gearing	35%
Income gearing	30%
RoCE	20%
Pretax profit margin	8%

The investors' ratios

The dividend is an important part of large investors' portfolio plans. The yield will therefore tend to be around the average for the sector and even for the whole market. The P/E is similarly near the average for the sector.

The dividend cover has gone sharply down as investors start to make the returns they were expecting at this stage in Compusell's life cycle.

COMPUSELL'S INVESTOR RATIOS AT STAGE 3

Yield	4%
Price/earnings	18
Dividend cover	1.9

Stage 4 – Over 25 years

Shareholders have now stopped looking for excitement in the share and want long-term promises on dividends and the delivery of these promises.

The company is in the Dow Jones 30 and has high-profile chairman and nonexecutive directors. You will hear its chairman frequently on the TV and radio talking about the company's performance, the economic situation, the competitive environment, and other current affairs. Using the naval example, the board is now commanding a battleship or a stately galleon.

The battleship analogy holds true in the length of time it takes to get a large company to react to problems. Suppose the market for your products becomes more competitive and prices have to come down to maintain sales volume. To protect your bottom line you have to cut costs, either direct (the cost of making the product) or indirect (administration and overheads).

A small business can make this happen immediately, whereas Compusell at this stage might take a year or more to make the correction, during which time we will see a lowering of the profit margin.

Representatives of the company now have a lot of power over standards bodies and supplier policies. Someone from Compusell is on the panel in any debate with a computer context from virtual reality shopping to home working.

The salesforce now has more "farmers" in it than "hunters." The company has well-founded key account management techniques in place to develop and protect market share. The third-party channels through which a large part of its sales go are encouraged by centrally devised marketing promotions and offers.

At this stage the chairman sometimes complains about the view which the stock market takes of Compusell's shares. The company likes to think it is a growth and innovation enterprise, while the market sees it as primarily a seller of commodity products, with limited opportunities for the sort of growth that will make a significant difference to its profit stream.

The annual report

There is an emphasis on benefits to customers in the report. The company takes very seriously its dominant place in a number of markets and is anxious to show that it is not exploiting this. Compusell will boast of new offerings to its customers, lower prices, and generally better service.

The following extracts are from the chairman's statement for a stage 4 company:

"Steady growth of sales, 4%, and earnings, 5.5%, demonstrate our progress towards meeting the expectations of both our share-holders and our customers."

"Against this economic and competitive background, Compusell's strategy remains clear. We will develop vigorously in our traditional markets and at the same time establish ourselves in new markets for our products and services both in our traditional areas and new parts of the world.''

The ratios

The ratios are all safer than the industry average and are at the top end of the benchmark. There is no question in the short term that the company can maintain its market and profit growth, limited though that is. Investors will be wary for any signs of decline. Regulations and new competitors represent the biggest risk.

Compusell has already shown good control of costs, but this needs to be a continuing phenomenon to remain reflected in the profit margins.

COMPUSELL'S RATIOS AT STAGE 4

Gearing	15%
Income gearing	20%
RoCE	25%
Pretax profit margin	10%

The investors' ratios

The share is now in almost all pension and private portfolios. The expectation is for dividend progress rather than capital growth and the yield and dividend cover show it. The yield is well above the average and cover is at a low level. Dividend cover probably wants to stay around here except if there is an exceptional item affecting profits.

The P/E is the sign of the stately galleon.

COMPUSELL'S INVESTOR RATIOS AT STAGE 4

Yield	5.9%
Price/earnings	13.8
Dividend cover	1.5

Here is a summary of Compusell's ratios over the four stages of its development. Whilst not a scientific benchmark, it provides a reasonable rule of thumb to make a preliminary judgment about any company. Look at the company's position in the stages of development, and then at its ratios. Look for inconsistencies with the benchmark and investigate from there.

COMPUSELL'S INVESTOR RATIOS
Compusell's ratios over the four stages

Gearing	75%	60%	35%	15%
Income gearing	95%	75%	30%	20%
RoCE	1%	10%	20%	25%
Pretax profit margin	1%	4%	8%	10%

Compusell's investor ratios over the four stages

Yield	0.3%	1.6%	4%	5.9%
Price/earnings	35	25	18	13.8
Dividend cover	13	3.5	1.9	1.5

NB This benchmark is viable when judged over the performance of companies and stock markets over many years. At the time of writing, price/earnings ratios have been, on average, at a much higher level and correspondingly yields have been much lower. Time will tell if low inflation and therefore relatively high P/Es are here to stay. We could add that volatility in the Compusell type of share has never been so high, no matter what stage of the company's development you examine.

Conclusion

Whilst recognizing that all businesses, and indeed all sectors, have different characteristics, we can already see pigeon-holes which we can use to distinguish one kind of company from another. They require little working out but are very helpful in determining the health of a company.

Investors, for example, have different requirements for the shares in their portfolio. Suppose you are about to retire. You want to use your share portfolio to protect your capital, i.e. take little risk, and live on the dividends the portfolio pays. In this case you will have a preponderance of Stage 4 companies in your portfolio.

This is not true of young high earners. They are paying income tax at the highest level and therefore do not need the dividend income. They are in no rush to turn the shares into cash and will therefore tend towards a portfolio of higher risk/higher return stage 1 companies.

Notice how easy it is to spot the type of company preferred if you have access to the three shareholder numbers and the four key ratios.

THE NOKIA – ERICSSON COMPARISON

The history of the mobile phone market has been one of outstanding growth, but in recent years it has matured very rapidly. This has brought problems for hitherto high growth companies. Nowhere is this more apparent than in the contrasting histories of Nokia and Ericsson, and in the way in which they have addressed the situation.

We can see this by comparing some of their key ratios. We have calculated one set of ratios based on the two companies' accounts for 1999 and one for the most recently available period, which covered 2004, and then put the numbers side by side in the following tables.

Ericsson is a good benchmark for Nokia, since it is also a Scandinavian company, but the numbers show that its financial position has been transformed over the years with some radical action. We also chose 1999 as the starting point, because it represented the peak of the dot.com bubble, close to the peak of the rapid growth phase of the mobile phone market, and a time when any manager could have made money in mobile phones. So how well were Nokia and Ericsson set up to counter the downturn?

All the information we need can be gleaned from their annual reports.

Nokia's R&D and the bottom line

The sheer competitiveness of the mobile market and the need to come up with new design features and innovations in turn suggests the companies need to spend significantly on research & development. In 1999, however, Nokia's spending on this area was significantly lower than Ericsson's. This might have suggested that Nokia was resting on its laurels to some degree. Had it, perhaps, grown complacent by the easy successes it had scored while the mobile phone market was growing rapidly?

Table 7.1

All currency numbers in €mn	Nokia 1999	Nokia 2004	Ericsson 1999	Ericsson 2004
R&D Spend	1755	3733	3354	2158
R&D Spend as a percentage of sales	8.8	12.8	13.2	15.5

At the time commentators appeared unconcerned about this, suggesting that while Nokia's spending might be less, it spent its money more effectively than its competitors. In hindsight, this reasoning appears to have been flawed. Nokia's products came to be seen as rather dated as other competitors stole a march with colour screens and camera phones.

Nokia's employees and the bottom line

At the end of the 1990s, Nokia was reckoned to have the most highly motivated workforce in the industry. But many commentators ignored the fact that, while the company's sales and profit per employee were high, the workforce was not rewarded commensurately, perhaps because of Nokia's position as a key employer in Finland.

In Sweden, by contrast, Ericsson paid more to its workforce, but generated less profit. The numbers show this clearly.

Now look at how this changed over the succeeding five years. Nokia lifted its wages per employee to more than Ericsson is now paying. Sales

Table 7.2

All currency numbers in €mn	Nokia 1999	Nokia 2004	Ericsson 1999	Ericsson 2004
Sales per employee	386435	546934	242941	276072
Profit per employee	75131	88000	19052	59386
Average wage per employee	38025	52419	41807	49906

and profit per employee are also significantly higher than they were back in 1999. But the same is true of Ericsson. Its wages per employee have risen significantly, but radical corporate restructuring (see later pages for an explanation of what has happened) have transformed profit per employee – raising the figure from €19,052 to €59,386. Though still less than Nokia's number, it is a remarkable transformation nonetheless.

Nokia – Inventory, payment and the bottom line

Take two other main indicators – stock turnover and the collection period. The first of these shows how effective the company is in making what its customers need and in selling it quickly. The second shows how quickly it collects payments due from customers.

Table 7.3

All currency numbers in €mn	Nokia 1999	Nokia 2004	Ericsson 1999	Ericsson 2004
Stock turnover	11.2	22.4	8.4	9.4
Collection period in days	70.6	54.6	107.7	90.3

This demonstrates Nokia has now recovered from the glitch that saw it lose favour with consumers (at the cost of writing down surplus inventory), and now turns over stock very rapidly indeed. Its payment collection period also shortened significantly between the two dates. The same is true for Ericsson, although the improvements, though good, are less marked.

Nokia – financing and the bottom line

Both companies have strong balance sheets. Table 7.4 shows how the capital and income gearing at both companies has fallen to zero. Both companies have cash balances that exceed their debt obligations while, by the same token, interest income is greater than interest paid in both cases. Ericsson shows much the biggest improvement largely because, as we explain in detail later, it has hived off its mobile phone business into a 50% owned joint venture. This has transformed the company's balance sheet, which was 62% geared in 1999. Nokia's gearing at the time was already very modest indeed.

Table 7.4

All currency numbers in €mn	Nokia 1999	Nokia 2004	Ericsson 1999	Ericsson 2004
Capital gearing	16.2	0	62.1	0
Income gearing	6.2	0	15.0	0

Nokia – margins (the real bottom line)

Now let's look at those all-important profit margins. Here again the story is one of massive improvement at Ericsson and a faltering at Nokia. This is shown in Table 7.5.

Table 7.5

All currency numbers in €mn	Nokia 1999	Nokia 2004	Ericsson 1999	Ericsson 2004
Sales	19722	29267	25500	13972
Cost of sales	12227	18133	14902	7490
Gross margin	38.2	38.0	41.6	46.3
Operating profit	3908	4330	2082	3059
Operating margin	19.8	14.8	8.2	21.9

Nokia's gross margin has remained solid over the period, at around 38%. It can still buy in materials and make phones on the same profit margin as before. The difference comes when you add in other operating costs, like R&D, employee costs, and other items. Here the picture is starkly different. Nokia's operating margins have fallen significantly, from 19.8% to 14.8% – a sign of the sharply increased competition it is now encountering.

At Ericsson, by contrast, the picture looks much better. Gross margin is up from 41.6% to 46.3%, while operating margins are up from 8.2% to 21.9%. Remember, however, that to some extent this is an accounting quirk. Because Ericsson's mobile phone business is now in a 50% joint venture, it takes in its share of profits as 'income from related companies', and does not include the turnover attributable to it. So while Ericsson deserves full marks for grasping the nettle and reorganizing, if we compare Nokia's margins with Ericsson's, we are not quite comparing like with like.

Most of Ericsson's profits now come from telephone systems while mobile phone assets and liabilities are no longer fully included in the balance sheet and profits are relegated to a contribution which amounts to little more than 10% of profits.

In 1999 Nokia and Ericsson were chasing different strategies. Nokia wanted volume and sales growth and market leadership in mobile phones was its key aim. Ericsson on the other hand was seeing its upstart mobile phone business contributing to profits for the first time, but still had big businesses in other areas. In the end, Ericsson concluded that it could only compete by joining forces with another player in the mobile business and the resulting joint venture with Sony has transformed the financial health of the company.

In the meantime Nokia has gone through a bad patch as a result its earlier seeming complacency, but now appears to have begun addressing its problems and is seeing an improvement. But it may yet regret becoming so dependent on the increasingly mature and consequently highly competitive mobile phone handset business.

The tortoise and the hare

In the end, companies have to generate acceptable returns for shareholders and will only survive as going concerns in the long term if they return more to shareholders than their underlying cost of capital.

Table 7.6 show return on capital employed and profit margins for both companies. Nokia's numbers betray the competitiveness of the mobile phone business. Return on capital is still an impressive 31%, but well down on the figure of five year ago. Over the same period Ericsson's ROCE has more than doubled to 29.4%. At the same time, Nokia's pretax margins have drifted from 19.4% to 16.1% while Ericsson's have risen from 7.8% to 21.5%. It is a real case of the tortoise and the hare.

Table 7.6

All currency numbers in €mn	Nokia 1999	Nokia 2004	Ericsson 1999	Ericsson 2004
Sales	19772	29267	25500	13972
Profit before tax	3845	4709	1999.8	3001
Profit margin	19.4	16.1	7.8	21.5
Return on capital employed	48.6	31.6	14.2	29.4

WHAT IS THE GOOD OF GOODWILL?

This book has unashamedly supported the calculations of those ratios that investors and directors have for many years seen as important. There are, of course, others, but to be honest they tend to come into fashion and then when the business environment has changed they tend to be quietly dropped. The danger here is that analysts change the ratios they regard as important to absolve a company with whose strategy they agree, but whose finances do not support that strategy measured by the old measures.

So how do you square the circle of appreciating a company's strategy but explain away, for example negative shareholders' equity after eliminating goodwill, or a lack of profitability on conventional profit calculations? Easy, invent another measure. Thus was born EBITDA. EBITDA disregards depreciation of fixed assets and amortization of goodwill on the slightly flaky grounds that they are merely "book entries" and do not involve any further actual cash expense. Even if you buy that for amortization of goodwill, it is hard to accept it for depreciating fixed assets. After all, these assets will probably have to be replaced when they are worn out if the company is to stay in business. Warren Buffet, a guru of investors, said that ignoring depreciation charges was akin to assuming that the tooth fairy would replace a company's plant and machinery. For completeness, however, here is how you calculate EBITDA.

EBITDA = pretax profit + interest paid + depreciation

+ amortization

People then use this number in various ways to support companies that are pursuing an acquisition policy, very fashionable in the late 1990s, which is incidentally the time when stock market evaluations got so out of synchronization with actual business performance that companies were being traded at P/E ratios that were over 80, and in some cases were more or less incalculable. Nonetheless EBITDA, which some waggish analysts call 'earnings before all the bad stuff' is still widely used when it is convenient to do so.

WATCHING FOR A CHANGE IN STRATEGY

We have said that it is not just the numbers that you need to examine to assess whether or not you are looking at a company that you wish to invest in, or work for, or sell to, or whatever. You also need to check the strategy, particularly when there has been a change of management.

Consider Marconi, formerly GEC. Before its share price collapsed in 2001, this one time industrial giant was valued at £35bn. As of late 2005, the bulk of the business had been sold to Ericsson for just £1.2bn. Could assiduous reading of the annual report have sounded a warning? Well, you would have seen the change in strategy and made a judgment on that. In 1996 you would have seen that George Simpson became the chief executive, replacing the long-time guru of British industry Lord Weinstock. Over the next few years Simpson dissipated the cash mountain that Weinstock had built up over the years as a prudent way of running a company with high-technology products. The City argued during Weinstock's time that he should have been more adventurous and invested that money rather than sitting on it.

Incidentally, Weinstock's answer to this was to say that the City did not understand business, and that they did not like him since he never went to them to pay them large fees for raising money from the market, since he already had quite enough of his own, thank you very much. He further argued that if you were in the business of selling trains that go through the channel tunnel using new technology, including 40 computers per train, it was wise to have a lot of cash to back your technologists up in case there was a problem.

So what did Simpson do? He decided to concentrate on the industry sector that had the greatest hope of strong profits growth, and therefore offered the best opportunity for the fast increase in the share price. This meant divesting the broad range of companies in the group that included defense, electrical engineering, advanced electronics, healthcare, and some others. This got down to the new core business of telecommunications. He then spent that money and the cash mountain on buying other companies in the industry at a time when the valuations of them were through the roof.

Investors could have spotted the change and changed their assessment of Marconi's risk. They could have seen how the old guard were systematically removed until all the executive directors were very much part of the *avant-garde*.

(In an article in *The Times* of July 9, 2001, William Rees-Mogg, for many years a nonexecutive director of GEC, revealed how it was hinted to him that he might leave the company before his time was up so that Simpson could bring in his own people. As Rees-Mogg queries, "His own team of executive directors?")

Investors would have seen the changes in the businesses in the company and the change to borrowing, and therefore gearing, from the interim and full-year reports. They could have taken profits or got out when the time was right.

If this last story sounds a little bitter, we ought to reveal an interest here. We bought GEC into our investment club some years ago when the company took its place in the low-risk part of the portfolio. We failed to keep up with the changes that were taking place and got burnt along with many other small investors.

INSIGHTS

When you are analyzing an annual report you need a benchmark. Compare one company with another in the same industry in order to be able to take a view on both of them. Remember to look at the strategy as well as the figures. Strategies do not stay the same forever, and you could be dealing with a very different kind of company over time, through radical changes in the strategy.

08

Key Concepts and Thinkers

This chapter encourages learning from the work of others and understanding the jargon of the strategy and finance side of the annual report, by including:

» descriptions of the work of four gurus and their impact;
» a glossary of terms.

"I know nothing except the fact of my ignorance."
Socrates (469–399 BC), Greek philosopher

KEY THINKERS

Company reports are a fashion business. Gurus come and go, but at least two have stood the test of time: one whose investment strategy is based on his prudent use of his knowledge of business, Warren Buffet, and another, Jim Slater, for his concentration on finding the winning formula for short-term investment gains. But perhaps the person who has had most impact on the way that figures have to be portrayed in the annual report is Terry Smith.

Warren Buffet

Warren Buffet is probably the most famous, and successful, thinker about investing in companies. His holding company Berkshire Hathaway has produced an enviable track record measured over the long term. His most notable success of recent years was during the huge fall in technology stocks that occurred in 1999/2000. How did he do it? Easy really, his investment strategy did not let him buy them in the first place. Buffet's technique is to look forward into the very long term. He looks for companies whose management he believes in and ones whose prospects for long-term success are good. He also wants to buy shares in companies where he can get enough to have a significant holding in the company. And his timescale is basically "forever."

He came under unusual amounts of criticism for the way this strategy kept him out of technology companies during the huge boom in the middle to late 1990s. He is reported as having said that he had "no insights into which companies in [the technology] field possess a truly durable competitive advantage." As a result of this, his fund hit its low at the same time as the NASDAQ index, the American index of companies in the technology sector, hit its high. Buffet had the last laugh, of course, with the NASDAQ plummeting while Berkshire Hathaway continued on its prosperous way with its portfolios of old economy companies. His fund is in brick making, building products, paint, and carpet making, to name but a few.

Jim Slater

Jim Slater invented a new ratio – the PEG. He considered that it is a better indicator than the P/E ratio or PER. The price earnings growth factor (PEG) is calculated by dividing the prospective PER of a share by the estimated future growth rate in earnings per share. Because it relates the PER of a company to the growth rate, Slater believes that it gives a better indicator of value. He believes that the PEG of a company is a more sophisticated measure than a PER.

On this basis he has produced works and tables that purport to give good tips on the right growth shares to buy. Frankly, like most insights into new ratios and methods of making investments, it can be proved to have worked at least some of the time in the past. Who knows, it may work again in the future; but it is left to the investor to work out, or guess, when that might be.

A lot of investors prefer to look at the underlying strategy of companies and compare their figures using more traditional financial ratios. After all, an investment is made to back a management team to be successful in the long term, not to use past experience in an attempt to forecast the future.

Terry Smith

The front page of Terry Smith's epoch-making book *Accounting for Growth*,[1] has a label across it saying "The book they tried to ban." The "they" in this remark referred to the various finance directors and their auditors whose accounting for growth practices the book exposed. In the introduction he quotes his many friends who asked him how a company that was reporting profits could go bust. Polly Peck is used as an example of the most dramatic and speedy collapse. Smith examines that in full and looks at other existing businesses in terms of their annual reports and what they hide. Thus "they" were upset.

He identified 12 types of obfuscation and poor accounting practices that made the company's position look healthier than it actually was. The techniques include off balance sheet finance and extraordinary and exceptional items reporting, both of which have had new accounting standards brought in to correct the potential problems.

He then draws a matrix of a large number of companies and indicates which of the 12 techniques their annual reports used. Finally he compares the usage of these techniques with the eventual share price collapse of constituent members of the list.

The lay person can understand most of what he writes, and though we do not agree with everything he says about reading an annual report (he says that you should start reading from the back, for instance), this book is still essential reading for people who want to understand the topic thoroughly.

I mean, have you ever tried to talk to a finance director? They talk in tongues.

Professor Sir David Tweedie

Many people credit Sir David Tweedie with picking up the weaknesses of current accounting standards, including those raised by Terry Smith, and striving to get a more accurate picture of a company represented in its annual report. He has certainly been very instrumental in pursuing a worldwide standard.

His credentials are impeccable. He was appointed to the International Accounting Standards Board in June 2000, effective January 1, 2001. Sir David was educated at Edinburgh University (B.Com, 1966; PhD, 1969) and qualified as a Scottish Chartered Accountant.

He was appointed technical director of the Institute of Chartered Accountants of Scotland in 1978 and moved from there in 1982 to the position of national technical partner of the then Thomson McLintock & Co. In 1987 his firm merged with Peat Marwick Mitchell & Co., at which time he was appointed national technical partner of KPMG Peat Marwick McLintock.

He was the UK and Irish representative on the International Auditing Practices Committee from 1983 to 1988 and chairman of the UK's Auditing Practices Committee from 1989 to 1990.

In 1990 he was appointed the first full-time chairman of the (then) newly created Accounting Standards Board, the committee charged with the responsibility for producing the UK's accounting standards, and in 1995 became a UK representative on the International Accounting Standards Committee (IASC). His appointment at the ASB ended in December 2000.

He is a visiting professor of accounting in the Management School at Edinburgh University. He has been awarded honorary degrees by six British Universities, the ICAEW's Founding Societies Centenary Award doctorate for 1997, and the CIMA Award 1998 for services to the accounting profession.

GLOSSARY OF TERMS

Accounting policies – Those principles and practices applied by an entity that specify how the effects of transactions and other events are to be reflected in the accounts. For example, an entity may have a policy of revaluing fixed assets or of maintaining them at historical cost. Accounting policies do not include estimation techniques.

Accounts payable – American terminology for creditors.

Accounts receivable – American terminology for debtors.

Accrual – An expense or a proportion thereof not invoiced prior to the balance sheet date but included in the accounts sometimes on an estimated basis.

Accruals concept – Income and expenses are recognized in the period in which they are earned or incurred, rather than the period in which they happen to be received or paid.

Asset – Any property or rights owned by the company that have a monetary value. In UK accounting standards, assets are defined as "rights or other access to future economic benefits controlled by an entity as a result of past transactions or events."

Balance sheet – A statement describing what a business owns and owes at a particular date.

Break-even point – The level of activity at which the fixed costs of a project are just covered by the contribution from sales. At this point there is neither a profit nor a loss.

Break-even analysis – A form of analysis that relates activity to totals of revenue and costs based on the classification of costs into fixed and variable.

Capital employed – The aggregate amount of long-term funds invested in or lent to the business and used by it in carrying out its operations.

Cash flow forecast – A statement of future, anticipated cash balances based on estimated cash inflows and outflows over a given period.

Cash flow statement – A statement of cash flows during the most recent accounting period. The required format for a cash flow statement is laid down in accounting standards.

Comparability – The requirement that once an accounting policy for a particular item in the accounts has been adopted, the same policy should be used from one period to the next. Any change in policy must be fully disclosed. Comparability is also important when comparing entities in the same industry. They should, wherever possible, use similar accounting policies.

Contingent liability – A possible obligation arising from past events whose existence will be confirmed only by the occurrence of one or more uncertain future events not wholly within the entity's control.

Costs of capital – The weighted average costs of funds to a company based on the mix of equity and loan capital and their respective costs. This is sometimes used as the required rate of return in a discounted cash flow.

Costs of good sold (or Cost of sales) – Those costs (usually raw materials, labor, and production overheads) directly attributable to goods that have been sold. The difference between sales and cost of goods sold is gross profit.

Creditors – Amounts due to those who have supplied goods or services to the business.

Current asset – An asset which, if not already in cash form, is expected to be converted into cash within 12 months of the balance sheet date.

Current cost – The convention by which assets are valued at the cost of replacement at the balance sheet date (net of depreciation for fixed assets).

Current liability – An amount owed which will have to be paid within 12 months of the balance sheet date.

Current ratio – The ratio of current assets to current liabilities in a balance sheet, providing a measure of business liquidity.

Debentures – Long-term loans, usually secured on the company's assets.

Debtors – Amounts due from customers to whom goods or services have been sold but for which they have not yet paid.

Deferred asset/liability – An amount receivable or payable more than 12 months after the balance sheet date.

Deferred taxation – An estimate of a tax liability payable at some estimated future date, resulting from timing differences in the taxation and accounting treatment of certain items of income and expenditure.

Depreciation – An estimate of the proportion of the cost of a fixed asset which has been consumed (whether through use, obsolescence, or the passage of time) during the accounting period.

Discounted cash flow (DCF) – A method of appraisal for investment projects. The total incremental stream of cash for a project is tested to assess the level of return it delivers to the investor. If the return exceeds the required, or hurdle, rate the project is recommended on financial terms or vice versa.

Distribution – The amount distributed to shareholders out of the profits of the company, usually in the form of a cash dividend.

Dividend cover – The ratio of the amount of profit reported for the year to the amount distributed.

Dividend yield – The ratio of the amount of dividend per share to the market share price of a listed company.

Earnings per share – The amount of profit (after tax and any extraordinary items) attributable to shareholders divided by the number of ordinary shares in issue.

EBIT – Earnings (profit) before interest and tax.

EBITDA – Earnings (profit) before interest, tax, depreciation and amortization. This measure of operating cash flow is considered to be an important measure of the performance of an entity.

Estimation techniques – The methods adopted by an entity to arrive at estimated monetary amounts for items in the accounts. For example, of the various methods that could be adopted for depreciation, the entity may select to depreciate using the straight-line method.

Exceptional item – Income or expenditure that, although arising from the ordinary course of business, is of such unusual size or incidence that it needs to be disclosed separately.

Expense – A cost incurred, or a proportion of a cost, the benefit of which is wholly used up in the earning of the revenue for a particular accounting period.

Extraordinary item – Material income or expenditure arising from outside the ordinary course of business. As a result of recent changes to accounting standards, it is considered that extraordinary items are extremely rare if not nonexistent.

Fixed asset – Asset held for use by the business rather than for sale.

Fixed cost – A cost that does not vary in proportion to changes in the scale of operations, e.g. rent.

Gearing – Gearing is the word used to describe the financing of the company in terms of the proportion of capital provided by shareholders (equity) compared with the proportion provided by loan capital (debt).

Gearing ratios – There are many different ways to measure gearing. The commonest is probably the ratio of debt to equity. That is the ratio of long-term loans to shareholders' funds (which can be measured in terms of nominal value or market value). Another common approach (called the capital gearing ratio) is to calculate the percentage of debt to total capital (debt plus equity). The income gearing ratio is the ratio of interest payable to the profits out of which interest is paid.

Gross profit – The difference between sales and the cost of goods sold.

Historic cost convention – The convention by which assets are valued on the basis of the original cost of acquiring or producing them.

Hurdle rate – The rate of return decided on by a company as the minimum acceptable for capital investment. It will be governed by the company's cost of capital and it may allow for different levels of risk.

Interest cover – The relationship between the amount of profit (before interest and before tax) and the amount of interest payable during a period.

Internal rate of return (IRR) – The rate of discount that equates the present values of all the cash inflows associated with an investment with its costs. The IRR is used to measure the return from a project where differing amounts of investment may be required at different times and where the returns and payback from it are spread unevenly.

It measures the effective yield on the investment. If this yield is greater than the hurdle rate the investment is seen to be financially desirable and vice versa.

Liability – An amount owed. In UK accounting standards, liabilities are defined as "an entity's obligations to transfer economic benefits as a result of past transactions or events."

Liquidity – A term used to describe the cash resources of a business and its ability to meet its short-term obligations.

Listed investments – Investments the market price for which is quoted on a recognized stock exchange. They may therefore be traded on that exchange.

Long-term liability – An amount payable more than 12 months after the balance sheet date.

Market price – The price of a quoted security for dealing in the open market.

Net assets – The amount of total assets less total liabilities.

Net book value – The cost (or valuation) of fixed assets less accumulated depreciation to date. Net book value bears no relationship to market value.

Net current assets – The amount of current assets less current liabilities.

Net present value (NPV) – A positive or negative value arrived at by discounting the cash flow from a capital project by the desired rate of return. If the value is positive, it means that the project is desirable and vice versa.

Net realizable value – Amount at which an asset could be sold in its existing condition at the balance sheet date, after deducting any costs to be incurred in disposing of it.

Nominal value – The face value of a share or other security.

Opportunity cost – The alternative advantage foregone as a result of the commitment of resources to one particular end.

Overhead – Any expense, other than the direct cost of materials or labor, involved in making a company's products.

Payback period – A term used in investment appraisal. It refers to the time required for the nondiscounted cash inflow to accumulate to the initial cash outflow in the investment.

Prepayment – The part of a cost which is carried forward as an asset in the balance sheet to be recognized as an expense in the ensuing period(s) in which the benefit will be derived from it, e.g. the payment in advance of rates.

Price/earnings ratio – The relationship between the market price of a share and its latest reported earnings per share.

Profit – The difference between the revenues earned in the period and the costs incurred in earning them. Alternative definitions are possible according to whether the figure is struck before or after tax.

Profit and loss account – A statement summarizing the revenues and the costs incurred in earning them during an accounting period.

Provision – A liability of uncertain timing or amount. A provision should only be recognized in the balance sheet when an entity has a present obligation (legal or constructive) as a result of a past event, it is probable that a transfer of economic benefits will be required to settle the obligation, and a reliable estimate can be made of the amount of the obligation. Unless these conditions are met, no provision should be recognized

Quick ratio – The ratio of those current assets readily convertible into cash (usually current assets less stock) to current liabilities.

Residual value – A notional cash inflow attributed to a capital project to allow for value remaining in the project at the final year of the assessment.

Revaluation reserve – The increase in value of a fixed asset as a result of a revaluation. This needs to be included in the balance sheet as part of shareholders' funds in order to make the balance sheet balance.

Revenue reserves – The accumulated amount of profit less losses generated by the company since its incorporation and retained in it. It is usually called "profit and loss account" in the balance sheet.

Revenue – Money received from selling the product of the business.

Sensitivity analysis – Analysis of the change in the output values of an equation by small changes to the input values. It is used to assess the risk in an investment project.

Share capital – Stated in the balance sheet at its nominal value and (if fully paid, and not subject to any share premium) representing the amount of money introduced into the company by its shareholders at the time the shares were issued.

Shareholders' funds – A measure of the shareholders' total interest in the company, represented by the total of share capital plus reserves.

Share premium – The surplus over and above nominal value received in consideration for the issue of shares.

Turnover – Revenue from sales.

Variable cost – A cost that increases or decreases in line with changes in the level of activity.

Working capital – Current assets less current liabilities, representing the amount a business needs to invest and which is continually circulating in order to finance its stock, debtors, and work in progress.

Work in progress – Goods (or services) in the course of production (or provision) at the balance sheet date.

NOTE

1 Smith, T. (1992) *Accounting for Growth*. Century Business, London.

09

Resources

Countless words have been written about the subject of financial reporting. This chapter gives descriptions of some useful sources of information, including:

» financial newspapers;
» analysts and web sites;
» books and articles.

"'That's not a regular rule; you invented it just now.'
'It's the oldest rule in the book,' said the King.
'Then it ought to be Number One,' said Alice."
Lewis Carroll (1832-98), in Alice's Adventures in Wonderland

NEWSPAPERS

Anyone trying to improve their knowledge of this topic needs to keep their learning up to date. By the time you have read this book, you will be able to pick up an annual report and in a fairly short time deliver an interpretation of the company's strategy and its financial position. The trouble is that if you do not do this exercise, or something like it, you will probably not be able to do that a month later.

The best, and probably most interesting, way to keep exercising your financial muscles is to read the finance pages of the newspapers or the specialist newspapers the *Financial Times* in the UK and the *Wall Street Journal* in the USA. Both of these papers are available all over the world.

Stock exchange listings

The *Wall Street Journal*, the *Financial Times* (*FT*), and many other newspapers carry a complete listing of the shares traded on one or more stock exchanges. In the *FT* you will find those companies on the London Stock Exchange and the Alternative Investment Market. In the *Wall Street Journal* you will find, amongst others, the main American markets - the New York Stock Exchange and NASDAQ.

We need to take examples for the purposes of this chapter, and we will take the *Financial Times* when discussing a fictitious recruitment company called HAR, and the *Wall Street Journal* when discussing a major computer supplier, also fictitious, Compusell.

The Financial Times

Towards the back of the 'companies and markets' section of the *FT* every day, there is a complete listing of the shares that are traded on the London Stock Exchange. This is a market where investors can buy and sell shares in listed companies. Buyers are people who want to start or increase a holding in a particular company and sellers are those who are holding shares which they bought earlier, either from a previous shareholder or directly from the company when the shares were initially issued.

Points to note. The listings are in industry sectors. This is done to ensure that readers are comparing like with like. It does not make sense to compare a telecomms company with a merchant bank. They are businesses with totally different characteristics.

Industry sectors

This sectorization is accepted in many other journals, and in business generally. It was extensively updated in late 1999 and modified later (see Fig. 9.1).

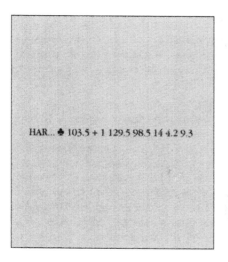

HAR... ♣ 103.5 + 1 129.5 98.5 14 4.2 9.3

Fig. 9.1 *Financial Times* listing for HAR.

The support services listings

If you go through HAR item by item, the first thing you see is an ace of clubs. Incidentally, the legend for all of these symbols is in the bottom right-hand column of the right-hand listings page.

The ace of clubs means that the company is part of the *FT* annual reports system. If you ring the telephone number mentioned or log on to its web site, it will send you the latest report of the company by post that day. It is a very efficient system.

We can now see the relevance of the price in pence. If 103.5 is the mid price, then the buying price will be about 105 and the selling price about 102. This is a spread of 3%.

Having said that, the percentage spread is actually a good deal lower for larger companies. Large companies have frequently traded shares and there is competition amongst marketmakers. In their case, the spread could be as little as 0.5%

xd

Beside the share price of a number of shares are the letters xd. You can see one of the companies above HAR, Capita, is xd right now. This stands for ex-dividend. This means that the shares are expected to pay a dividend shortly. But it also signifies that those buying the shares now will not be entitled to this payment, but only to subsequent ones.

Price movement

Continuing across the page, the next column shows the movement in the share during the previous day's trading. In this case HAR went up 1 pence between start and close of business yesterday.

Now for the year's high and low. During the last 52 weeks HAR has been trading at a high of 129.5 and a low of 98.5: a good demonstration of the volatility of shares. Equities do go sharply up and down in value. Sometimes because the whole market moves sharply, and sometimes because the individual share itself has been revalued by the market because of some event in the business.

Volume, in thousands ('000s)

The next piece of information is the volume of shares traded yesterday. This basically comments on how seriously any price movement should be taken.

The *FT* records both the selling and buying sides of the transaction, so the number of shares involved is half of the quoted figure. Only 7000 shares in HAR changed hands yesterday, causing a small shift in the price.

Yield

Back to the dividend return on investment. The yield for HAR is 1.8. This is a percentage and reflects the dividend return you can expect if you buy the shares at today's price, 103.5, and the company pays the same amount in dividend as it did last year. In other words last year's dividend payment (including any tax credit associated with it) represents, in this example, 1.8% of the current share price.

This last point is the complicating factor. Unless they have other information from published or other sources, a new investor in a company will expect the mangers to maintain or increase the annual dividend. They can only do this, of course, if they have the profits and cash to do so. When a yield suddenly goes very high, it means that the share price has dropped significantly, and that often means that investors, that is the market, are unsure whether the dividend will be maintained either now or in the future.

Price/earnings

The final number in the HAR entry is the P/E ratio. It stands at 9.3. From what you already know, this means that the total value of all the HAR shares when the price of each share is 103.5, is 9.3 times last year's earnings. The term 'Earnings' in this context means profits attributable to shareholders divided by the number of outstanding issued shares in the company.

Sector averages

Having the bald numbers of the yield percentage and the P/E multiple is only useful if there is a benchmark to compare them with. The benchmark supplied on a daily basis by the *FT* is that of the average for the sector.

On the back page of the companies and markets part of the *FT* there is a list of all the business sectors used in the listings page. Against each there is a lot of information calculated as an average of a number of companies in the sector. Included in these is yield and P/E.

The *Wall Street Journal*

Before moving on to look at what the other pages in the *FT* cover, let's take time out to examine one of the USA equivalents to the *FT* – the

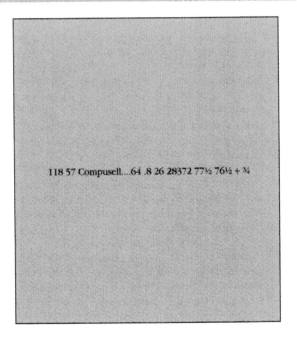

118 57 Compusell....64 .8 26 28372 77½ 76½ + ¾

Fig. 9.2 *Wall Street Journal* listing for Compusell.

Wall Street Journal. The information covered is similar to the *FT* but set out differently.

The first part of the entry is the 52-week high and low. The name of the stock is followed by the dividend in dollars. From this and the current price we could work out the yield, but the paper does this for us in the next column. So with Compusell the high for the year is 118 and the low 57. The dividend was 64 cents per share last year giving a yield of 0.8%.

The P/E ratio follows, which at 26 is at the low end of recent fluctuations. Now comes the volume of transactions yesterday in thousands ('000s).

There is now some information that is not given in the *FT*. The next two columns show the high and low prices reached during the day – these are called the intra-day high and low. Finally we get the share price with the change that occurred during the previous day.

There are many share indices quoted in the *Wall Street Journal*, of which the most famous are the Dow Jones Industrial Average and the Standards and Poor 500.

The other pages

At this stage we will just have a quick look at the other pages. The *FT* and the *Wall Street Journal* cover a lot of stories about mergers, take-overs, and things to do with the financing and ownership of businesses.

Notice the index at the bottom left-hand corner of the front page of the companies section of the *FT*. The paper is well indexed and most stories are trailed in one way or another. This greatly assists the reading of the paper since it is quite simple to pick out the parts that are of relevance to you because they affect your company, competitors, customers, or suppliers. In this way you can study your industry sector quickly by using the index.

Here is, from the archives of the late 1980s, information derived from an article about British Airways. Though this is a long time ago, it gives a good illustration of just how much you can learn from a short article.

THE WORLD'S FAVORITE AIRLINE

This is a good illustration of what we get out of reading the financial pages.

Economic news – One of the ways that companies economize during a period of slow growth is to limit the travel budgets of their employees. This saving comes through to BA as a reduction in the people paying premium rates to sit in business class rather than economy.

Currency news – The yen has strengthened against sterling. BA is either badly prepared for this or has used the yen to hedge against other currency changes. The result is that BA has an exposure of some £790m in yen finance that it has used to buy aircraft. This will cause a charge to the second quarter accounts of some £69m.

Industrial news - The report says that BA had been seeking a reduction of £42m in the wages bill for cabin crew. The staff responded to the threat to sack 1000 people by industrial disruption, hundreds of people calling in sick, and thwarted the sackings.

Commodity news - The rise in aviation fuel prices continues with the price of a tonne going from $165 to $200. BA has hedged this by buying forward almost 70% of the fuel it needs for the second half of the year.

Financial news - BA's first quarter profits fell 45.6% to £94m compared to last year. It was this announcement that triggered off the article. It is further reported that analysts are expecting the airline to do no better than break even this year compared to making a profit of £225m last year.

Strategy news - The article includes the airline's ideas for what it is going to do strategically about the situation. It intends to buy smaller aircraft in the future, which have a higher ratio of business class seats, which have a higher profit margin than economy seats. Further, it intends to counter accusations of overcharging for flights in Europe by offering another cheap fares promotion. Finally it is still looking for cost savings of £225m this year and to achieve this is going to chop 10% of its managers, putting some 1000 people off its books. This saving will cost £40 million to implement in redundancy and other charges. This gives the subeditor the headline "BA to cut 1000 jobs as it seeks cost savings of £225m."

All this information was available from a 10-column-inch article.

ANALYSTS

The clients of stockbrokers can use what is known as an execution only service. This is the cheapest way of using stockbrokers since they merely process the transaction you request, and have no part in advising you which shares you should buy or sell.

Alternatively you can ask stockbrokers for their advisory service and they will make recommendations for you to follow or reject. They do this, of course, for a fee. You can choose to have the stockbroker run the whole portfolio and have no part in the decision-making process at all. This tends to be the most expensive way of operating. It is called a 'discretionary' service, because the broker can act at his discretion on your behalf.

In the same way, companies hire groups of fund managers to run the huge portfolios in the company pension scheme.

All of this creates a demand for people who become expert in particular market sectors by studying the companies and their products and markets over long periods of time. Such analysts publish their findings. These are given free of charge to the firm's best clients, but it eventually the information finds its way into the papers.

There are many analysts offering their services online. For an introduction you might try www.barclays.co.uk. Almost all the leading stockbrokers and company information sites include information on their analyst service.

BOOKS

There is no shortage of material written about the topic of detecting the health and future prospects for companies. From penny share tip sheets (one has to wonder why the publishers bother sharing their secrets) to mighty academic tomes. If, for example, you are interested in taking your knowledge of investment forward, then this book of Buffet essays covers a lot of interesting ground.

Cunningham, L. (2000) *The Essays of Warren Buffet*. John Wiley and Sons, New York.

I. Corporate governance

» Owner-related business principles
» Boards and managers
» The anxieties of plant closing
» An owner-based approach to corporate charity
» A principled approach to executive pay

II. Corporate finance and investing
» Mr. Market
» Arbitrage
» Debunking standard dogma
» "Value" investing: a redundancy
» Intelligent investing
» Cigar butts and the institutional imperative
» Junk bonds
» Zero-coupon bonds
» Preferred stock

III. Common stock
» Bane of trading: transaction costs
» Attracting the right sort of investor
» Dividend policy
» Stock splits and trading activity
» Shareholder strategies
» Berkshire's recapitalization

IV. Mergers and acquisitions
» Bad motives and high prices
» Sensible stock repurchases versus greenmail
» Leveraged buy-outs
» Sound acquisitions policies
» On selling one's business

V. Accounting and taxation
» A satire on accounting shenanigans
» Look through earnings
» Economic goodwill versus accounting goodwill
» Owner earnings and the cash flow fallacy
» Intrinsic value, book value, and market price
» Segment data and consolidation
» Deferred taxes
» Retiree benefits and stock options
» Distribution of the corporate tax burden
» Taxation and investment philosophy

KEY LEARNING POINTS

A regular, perhaps weekly, reading of a specialist business paper is an effective way of developing and maintaining your financial knowledge. The stories in these pages also keep you up to date with the business environment and provide detailed information on industry sectors in which you have an interest. If you want to cover many of the issues that face an investor, you will get a lot of practical thinking out of *The Essays of Warren Buffet*.

Ten Steps to Understanding Accounts

Financial theory is one thing; putting it into practice another. Chapter 10 provides some key insights into making a useful a model to compare one company with another and with a benchmark, using the following steps:

1 first catch your report;
2 get an overview or feel;
3 think about the industry sector;
4 read the chairman's statement;
5 fill in the activity matrix;
6 understand the profit and loss account;
7 understand the balance sheet;
8 interpret the results;
9 build an industry average;
10 gather additional information from the company's web site.

"Annual income twenty pounds, annual expenditure nineteen nineteen six, result happiness. Annual income twenty pounds, annual expenditure twenty pounds ought and six, result misery."
Charles Dickens (1812-70), in David Copperfield

So now we need to pull everything together in a 10-step strategy for conveying the essential messages of an annual report to you as a businessperson or investor. Here first is our objective and the main principles.

PURPOSE (WHY)

To learn about the financial situation of a company by using published material.

PRINCIPLES

» Using this model gives a consistent measure and makes sure that you are comparing apples with apples.
» The directors' statements give a well-presented advertisement for the company. The figures tell the underlying story.
» Frequent use of this tool keeps the financial side of managing a business in the forefront of the mind.

1. FIRST CATCH YOUR REPORT

The easiest way of getting an annual report is to ring the company up and ask the switchboard. They will generally put you through to a shareholder support department, if it is a big company, or take your name and address there and then. In a smaller company you may be put through to the company secretary. I have yet to find a company not happy to send the report by return.

There are various publications that help you to find out the number of any UK listed company. The one a lot of people use is the *Pinsents Company Guide* published by HS Finance Publishing. Indeed, if you are looking for a short financial statement about a company, and you understand the ratios talked about in this book, you may find that this quarterly publication will give you all you need. You can get in contact with them on www.hsfinancial.com.

Alternatively, particularly if you want a number of reports, you can use the *Financial Times* newspaper's free annual report system. If the entry the company has in the listings section of the paper has the right symbol, currently the ace of clubs, then you can telephone the *FT* number given in the legend and you will be sent the report. You can also order reports on the *FT* web site, www.FT.com.

2. GET AN OVERVIEW OR FEEL

Consider the report in the first place for its extravagance. It must be very professional of course, but they are expensive to produce, and one is tempted to regard a particularly glossy one as presentation possibly being used to distract from the substance.

Now look at the financial highlights on the first or second page. This gives you a picture of the size of the company by turnover, and its position from last year to this. Now look at the growth of the profits. You will probably be able in your head to see if the growth of sales is matched by the growth in profits. If profit growth is higher than sales growth, this is a good sign and you will expect to read what has occurred to make this happen. If the company has increased sales at the cost of a diminishing profit margin, then you should expect to read in the report why this happened and how the managers are going to put it right.

In many reports there will be a highlight made of these two growth figures. Be careful with them. If you use the model in this book for all the analyses that you do, you will at least be consistent. The people who prepare annual reports are in a position to choose a version of the profit that suits them and the story they are trying to tell. If they got better growth in earnings per share, or profit after tax than in net profit before tax, they may well highlight one of those. Alternatively, they may choose to concentrate on profit before amortization. We will always use net profit before tax for comparative purposes.

3. THINK ABOUT THE INDUSTRY SECTOR

Be careful not to compare apples with pears. Industry sectors differ from each other and differ over time. What are the biggest issues facing that sector at this time? Is it a growth area, or is it at the consolidation stage of a mature business? Who are its main competitors, and is this likely to change in the short term? How does fashion affect this sector?

Ask a lot of similar open questions to get a feel for the sector. If you want to go deeper into this, you may want to look at Dun and Bradstreet reports on the sector, or its industry averages books. See www.DNB.com

4. READ THE CHAIRMAN'S STATEMENT

There is no document that a company produces that has more care lavished on it than the chairman's statement in the annual report. Your concentration at this step should give you a firm idea of where he or she is trying to take the business. Get your mind round the strategy, what businesses the company will be in in the future, and what their finances need to look like to support that strategy.

5. FILL IN THE ACTIVITY MATRIX

Now fill in the activity matrix in Figure 10.1. This tells you in a short diagram what the chairman and other directors see as their main product/markets. You can then make a judgment on those. You may wish to work out where the main product/market emphasis is going in the future according to the report. Do you agree with that strategy?

Activity matrix	Market 1	Market 2	Market 3	Market 4	Market 5	Market 6	Market 7	Market 8
Product 1								
Product 2								
Product 3								
Product 4								
Product 5								

Fig. 10.1 The activity matrix.

Table 10.1

Ref.	Term	Explanation	Comment
A	Sales	Sales outside the group excluding VAT	Also known as: Net sales Sales turnover Sales revenue
B	Net profit before tax	This is the profit before charging tax or extraordinary items	Almost always uses these words on the profit and loss account
C	Interest payable	Gross interest payable	Often on the balance sheet it shows net interest. The notes will give the gross figure payable
D	Depreciation	A method by which the full cost of an asset is charged against profit over the useful life of the asset	Can often be found on the cash flow statement or notes to it

6. UNDERSTAND THE PROFIT AND LOSS ACCOUNT

Figures you need to input are shown in Table 10.1.

7. UNDERSTAND THE BALANCE SHEET

Figures you need to input are shown in Table 10.2.

Figures calculated by the model from the information in Table 10.2 are shown in Table 10.3.

8. INTERPRET THE RESULTS

Key business ratios – profitability

See Table 10.4.

Key business ratios – liquidity

See Table 10.5.

Table 10.2

Ref.	Term	Explanation	Comment
E	Tangible fixed assets	Those assets, such as property, machinery, etc., that a company uses to generate income over a long period	Use the amount shown on the face of the balance sheet
F	Intangible fixed assets	Fixed assets without physical substance, such as licences, goodwill, and patents	Many balance sheets do not include any intangible assets
G	Other fixed assets	Assets that are neither of the above	Predominantly these are investments and trade investments
H	Stocks	Trading and other stocks, including raw materials, work in progress, and finished goods	Also known as: "inventory"
I	Trade debtors	Amounts receivable from customers. The balance sheet often has "debtors" and you have to go to the note to separate out trade debtors	Accounts receivable
J	Total current assets	The sum of all those assets that would normally be turned into cash within one year	
K	Trade creditors	Amounts owed to suppliers. The balance sheet often has "creditors" and you have to go to the note to separate out trade creditors	Accounts payable
L	Short-term loans	Loans payable within one year. This will include overdrafts and obligations under leases	There is often only one line to indicate all the short-term liabilities: "creditors: amounts due within one year"

Table 10.2 (*Continued*).

Ref.	Term	Explanation	Comment
M	Total current liabilities	The sum of all those liabilities that have to be paid within one year	Also known as "creditors: amounts due within one year"
N	Long term loans	Loans repayable after more than one year	
O	Provisions for liabilities and charges	Includes deferred tax and other provisions	
P	Other long term liabilities	Any other long-term liability not yet transferred to the tool	If you have had to go to the notes for the break down of long term liabilities, make sure you have transferred any liabilities not covered by the previous two items
Q	Total shareholders funds	The total of funds belonging to the shareholders, including undistributed profits, known as reserves	Use the figure described as the total
R	Minority interests	The amount of reserves that belongs to shareholders in nonwholly-owned subsidiaries	Quite often there are no minority interests
S	Average number of employees	Make sure you express this figure in the same units as the other figures	If, for example, the units used are £m, then 55,367 employees would be input as .055367
T	Employees remuneration	Wages and salaries, not including social security or pension costs	There is no requirement to give this number in the USA, so many companies do not

Table 10.3

Ref.	Term	Explanation	Comment
AA	Total fixed assets $= E + F$	Tangible fixed assets plus intangible fixed assets	
BB	Total assets $= E + F + G + J$	The sum of the book value of all assets owned by the company	
CC	Total liabilities $= M + N + O + P + R$	Total current liabilities plus long-term loans and other long-term liabilities including provisions and minority interests	
DD	Net assets $= BB - M$	Total assets less current liabilities	This figure is often given on the balance sheet, so you can use it to check your input
EE	Capital employed $= N + O + P + Q + R$	Represents capital employed in the company from shareholders and other long-term sources	Check that net assets (DD) equals this number. If it does not, you have made a mistake at the input stage
FF	Quick assets $= J - H$	Total current assets minus stock, gives those current assets that can definitely be turned into cash quickly	

Table 10.3 (*Continued*).

Ref.	Term	Explanation	Comment
GG	Total debt = L + N	Total loans outstanding - short plus long term	
HH	Net worth = Q − F	Shareholders' funds less intangible assets	Intangible assets may be suspect, so some ratios will be calculated form net worth
II	Preinterest profit = B + C	Profit available to meet the demands of shareholders and the providers of loans. Often described as EBIT – earnings before interest and tax	Earnings and profits have the same meaning in this context
JJ	Net working capital = J − M	Total current assets less total current liabilities	This is money tied up in the business, and shareholders want it to go round the working capital cycle as fast as possible

Table 10.4

Ref.	Term	Explanation	Comment
P1	Return on capital employed = B/EE	Preinterest profits expressed as a percentage of capital employed	One of the most important ratios, showing how well the directors are using the shareholders' funds
P2	Profit margin B/A	Pretax profit expressed as a percentage of sales	
P3	Return on assets = B/BB	Preinterest profits expressed as a percentage of total assets	
P4	Shareholders' return = B/HH	After tax profits expressed as a percentage of tangible net worth	

Table 10.5

Ref.	Term	Explanation	Comment
L1	Current ratio = J/M	The ratio of current assets to current liabilities	
L2	Quick ratio = FF/M	The ratio of current assets less stock to current liabilities	Also known as the acid test

Key business ratios – asset utility
See Table 10.6.

Key business ratios – gearing
See Table 10.7.

Key business ratios – employee
See Table 10.8.

Table 10.6

Ref.	Term	Explanation	Comment
A1	Stock turnover = A/H	The number of times stock is turned over during a year	Sometimes calculated as the number of days stock is held on average
A2	Collection period $365 \times$ I/A	The average amount of time expressed in days that customers take to pay invoices	
A3	Asset turnover = A/BB	Sales as a percentage of total assets	Sometimes called asset utilization

Table 10.7

Ref.	Term	Explanation	Comment
G1	Capital gearing = N/Q + N	A comparison of debt with total capital employed being shareholders' funds plus debt	High gearing, where there is a lot of debt, can be exciting but can make a company vulnerable to, for example, a slight decrease in sales or a small rise in interest rates
G2	Income gearing = C/II	Interest as a percentage of preinterest profit	How much of the company's profits does it take to pay the interest bill? Many see this as the key gearing ratio

Table 10.8

Ref.	Term	Explanation	Comment
E1	Sales per employee = A/S	Sales divided by employees	Shows how productive the employees are in generating sales
E2	Profit per employee = B/S	Pretax profits divided by employees	Shows how productive the employees are in generating profits
E3	Average wage per employee = T/S	Employee remuneration divided by the number of employees	Checks how competitive the company is in paying staff

Table 10.9

Ref.	Term	Explanation	Comment
S1	Sales growth	This calculation subtracts the previous year figure from the current year and expresses the result as a percentage of the previous year	
S2	Profit growth	This calculation subtracts the previous year figure from the current year and expresses the result as a percentage of the previous year	

Key business ratios – growth

See Table 10.9.

9. BUILD AN INDUSTRY AVERAGE

Previously we have mentioned that you can buy industry average material from business information suppliers such as Dun and Bradstreet.

It is, of course, cheaper to do this for yourself. Get hold of, say, five reports of companies that you wish to study from the same industry. Fill in the model for all five, and then add together the accumulated items, the total of all the sales turnover figures for example. You will probably have some difficulty in finding companies that match each other identically. If, in this case, a company has a division that is in quite a different sector, you should strip the figures for that division out. With some thought you will be able to make sure that you are comparing apples with apples.

Then compare the company you are particularly interested in and see how it is doing against the industry average.

10. GATHER ADDITIONAL INFORMATION FROM THE COMPANY WEB SITE

Company web sites contain a wealth of additional information about a company, and often include presentations and speeches made by company management, analyst forecasts, press releases, articles about the company, and other features. More important perhaps, they are a good way of getting a feel for the company's style and its general efficiency. A badly designed, poorly updated site speaks volumes.

KEY LEARNING POINTS

The way to become familiar and confident about reading and understanding accounts is to do the exercise regularly and frequently to begin with. Use the 10-step plan to carry this out.

Frequently Asked Questions (FAQs)

Q1: Can I pick up a company's report and within ten minutes know what their principal products and markets will be during the next 12 months?

A: See Chapter 10.

Q2: Do I know how to test whether a company's published strategy is financially viable?

A: See Chapter 6.

Q3: Can I define the most popularly quoted measures of profitability, liquidity, asset utility and gearing?

A: See Chapter 6.

Q4: Can I get the information from financial information published in an annual report, such as the profit and loss account and balance sheet, and calculate these popular measures of financial health?

A: See Chapter 10.

Q5: Can I explain to a nonfinancial manager how a company can be making a satisfactory return on investment but still be in danger of financial collapse?

A: See Chapter 9.

Q6: Can I access on the Internet figures that enable me to compare a company's financial measures with an industry average?

A: See Chapter 9.

Q7: Do I know how to make a proper comparison between US and European financial jargon?

A: See Chapter 8.

Q8: Do I understand which figures in a report and accounts are written to a global standard?

A: See Chapter 5.

Q9: Do I understand the significance of the words the auditors use in giving their opinion of the picture the financial figures paint of the company in question?

A: See Chapter 2.

Q10: Do I have access to tools to help keep my financial knowledge and skills up to date on a regular basis?

A: See Chapter 10.

Index

Accounting for Growth   81
Accounting Standards Board (ASB)
  33, 82
accounts   2-3, 6, 16
accruals concept   41, 83
acquisitions   19-20, 76
activity matrix   11, 106
administrative overheads   43
advertising   6, 19
analysts   98-9
annual reports   6-12, 93-4, 105
ASB *see* Accounting Standards Board
assets   44-6, 74-5, 113
audits   12, 16

balance sheets   18-9, 43-7, 83,
  107-11
Barnevik, Percy   30
bartering   14
bookkeeping   16-19
books   99-100
branding   30-31
British Airways article   97-8
Buffet, Warren   76, 80, 99

capital
  expenditure   40, 49

gearing   52-3, 73
  shareholders   38
  structures   20
  working cycle   38-40, 89
case studies
  Compusell   59-70
  Nokia/Ericsson   70-75
cashflow statements   47-50, 84
chairman's statement   8-9, 106
change   64, 76-8
chief executive reports   9-10
collection periods   72
Companies Acts (UK)   23, 33
comparability   84
competition   24-5
competitive advantage   9, 40, 80
Compusell case study   59-70
computers   17-18
concepts   83-9
convertible loan stock   16
cost of sales   42
creative accounting   6
creditors   10, 40, 46
credits   17
cultural issues   30-31
Cunningham, L.   99
customers   67-8, 72

debentures   84
debits   17
debt problems   6
depreciation   40-41, 46, 48, 85
direct cost *see* cost of sales
directors   9-12
distribution/selling expenses   43
dividend cover   61-9
dividends   8-9, 49, 58-9
donations   10
double-entry bookkeeping   17
Dun and Bradstreet ratings agency 114

e-trading   22-3
earn outs   19
earnings before interest, tax, depreciation and amortization (EBITDA)   75-6, 85
earnings per share   59
earnings statements   41, 43
EBITDA *see* earnings before interest, tax, depreciation and amortization
electronic publishing   23-4
employees   71-2, 114
equities   16
Ericsson/Nokia case study   70-75
The Essays of Warren Buffet   99
estimation   85
evolution   13-20
ex-dividend (xd)   94
expectations   7
expenditure   40, 49
expenses   43

Financial Accounting Standards Board (FASB)   32-3, 35
Financial Times (FT)   92-96, 105
four key ratios   50-55
fraud   17-18

frequently asked questions (FAQs) 117-18
FT see Financial Times
funds   47, 52, 89

gearing   52-4, 63-9, 73, 113
general business model   38-41
glossary   83-9
Goldstein-Jackson, Kevin   18
goodwill   45, 75-6
gross margins   42-3, 73-4
growth table   114

head offices   31-2
highlights   7-8, 105
history   13-20

IASB *see* International Accounting Standards Board
IASC *see* International Accounting Standards Committee
IASs *see* International Accounting Standards
income gearing   53-4, 73
income statements   18
indexes   97
industry averages   114-15
industry sectors   93, 105-6
information sharing   24-5
interest payable   53-4
internal rate of return (IRR)   86-7
International Accounting Standards Board (IASB)   33-6, 82
International Accounting Standards Committee (IASC)   35-6, 82
International Accounting Standards (IASs)   33-5
international standards   33-5
Internet   18, 22
intra day highs/lows   97
intranets   24-5
investor ratios   58-69

IOSCO *see* International Organisation
  of Securities Commissions
IRR *see* internal rate of return

jargon   3
Joint Stock Companies Act (USA)
  15-16

key aspects
  concepts   83-9
  frequently asked questions
    117-18
  glossary   83-9
  resources   92-101
  ten steps   104-15
  thinkers   80-83
knowledge centers   25-6

labor   39-40
learning   25-6
ledgers   17
legislation   16
*Lehmann Communications
  Company Guide*   104
liabilities   44, 46-7, 87
limited liability   15-16
liquidity   87, 112
loans   15, 46
Luce, Henry R.   14

management   3, 31, 64, 76
Marconi   76-7
margins   42-3, 73-5
market segmentation   11
matrix management   32
mergers   19-20
mission statements   7
money, four functions   14-15

newspapers   96-8
Nokia/Ericsson case study   70-75
nominal share values   16

operating margins   74
operations review   10-11
overheads   43
overview   105

P/E *see* price/earnings ratios
Paciolito, Luca   17
PEG *see* price earnings growth factor
Polly Peck   2, 81
pretax profit margins   55, 63-69
price earnings growth factor (PEG)
  81
price/earnings ratio (P/E)   59-69,
  76, 95-6
products   11
profits
  margins   42-3, 73-4
  pretax profit margins   55
  profit and loss accounts   41-3,
    107
  reserved profits   3
  retained profits   43, 47
  return on capital employed   54-5
  table   112
  trading   43
  warnings   7
promotional issues   23-4
propaganda   6

R&D *see* research and development
ratios   50-55, 58-69, 75
Rees-Mogg, William   77
reorganization   65
reports   6-12, 23-4, 93-4, 105
research and development (R&D)   9,
  71
reserved profits   3
resources   92-101
responsibilities   11-12
retained profit   43, 47
retirees   70

return on capital employed (RoCE)
54-5, 63-9, 75
review of operations   10-11
risks   62, 64
RoCE *see* return on capital employed

sales turnover   41-2
salespeople   30, 60
sector averages   95
Securities and Exchange Commission
(USA)   33
security   22
selling/distribution expenses   43
shareholders
capital   38
expectations   7
funds   47, 52, 89
ratios   51, 58-69
rights   2
shares   10, 16, 94, 96-7
Simpson, George   76-7
Slater, Jim   81
Smith, Terry   81
standardization   31, 35-6
standards   16, 32-6
statements
cashflow   84

chairman's statement   8-9, 106
income   18
mission   7
stewardship   16-17
stock   39, 44, 72-3
strategies   10, 75-8
structures   9, 20, 31

taxation   19, 49
technology   65
thinkers   80-83
trading   8, 43
training   31
transaction charges   22
Tweedie, Professor Sir David   33, 36,
82

Wall Street Journal   92, 96-8
warnings   7
Websites
electronic publishing   23-4
Weinstock, Lord   76-7
working capital cycle   38-40, 89

xd *see* ex-dividend

yield   58-69, 95-6
young high earners   70